GLOBALVIEWPOINTS

I Oil

DISCARD

Other Books of Related Interest:

At Issue Series

Ethanol

Introducing Issues with Opposing Viewpoints Series

Nuclear Power

Opposing Viewpoints Series

The Environment

Global Warming

GLOBALVIEWPOINTS

Oil

Margaret Haerens, Book Editor

GREENHAVEN PRESS
A part of Gale, Cengage Learning

GALE
CENGAGE Learning™

Detroit • New York • San Francisco • New Haven, Conn • Waterville, Maine • London

Christine Nasso, *Publisher*
Elizabeth Des Chenes, *Managing Editor*

© 2010 Greenhaven Press, a part of Gale, Cengage Learning

LIBRARY OF CONGRESS CATALOGING-IN-PUBLICATION DATA

Oil / Margaret Haerens, book editor.
   p. cm. -- (Global viewpoints)
   Includes bibliographical references and index.
   ISBN 978-0-7377-4719-5 (hbk.) -- ISBN 978-0-7377-4720-1 (pbk.)
   1. Petroleum reserves--Juvenile literature. 2. Petroleum industry and trade--Juvenile literature. 3. Energy consumption--Juvenile literature. I. Haerens, Margaret.
   HD9565.O552 2010
   333.8'232--dc22

                                     2009052251

Printed in the United States of America
1 2 3 4 5 6 7 14 13 12 11 10

Contents

Chapter 2: Oil and the Environment

Chapter 3: Oil and Politics

Chapter 4: Drilling for New Sources of Oil

Foreword

*"The problems of all of humanity can
only be solved by all of humanity."*
—Swiss author Friedrich Dürrenmatt

Global interdependence has become an undeniable reality. Mass media and technology have increased worldwide access to information and created a society of global citizens. Understanding and navigating this global community is a challenge, requiring a high degree of information literacy and a new level of learning sophistication.

Building on the success of its flagship series, *Opposing Viewpoints*, Greenhaven Press has created the *Global Viewpoints* series to examine a broad range of current, often controversial topics of worldwide importance from a variety of international perspectives. Providing students and other readers with the information they need to explore global connections and think critically about worldwide implications, each *Global Viewpoints* volume offers a panoramic view of a topic of widespread significance.

Drugs, famine, immigration—a broad, international treatment is essential to do justice to social, environmental, health, and political issues such as these. Junior high, high school, and early college students, as well as general readers, can all use *Global Viewpoints* anthologies to discern the complexities relating to each issue. Readers will be able to examine unique national perspectives while, at the same time, appreciating the interconnectedness that global priorities bring to all nations and cultures.

Material in each volume is selected from a diverse range of sources, including journals, magazines, newspapers, nonfiction books, speeches, government documents, pamphlets, organization newsletters, and position papers. *Global Viewpoints* is truly global, with material drawn primarily from international sources available in English and secondarily from U.S. sources with extensive international coverage.

Features of each volume in the *Global Viewpoints* series include:

- An **annotated table of contents** that provides a brief summary of each essay in the volume, including the name of the country or area covered in the essay.

- An **introduction** specific to the volume topic.

- A **world map** to help readers locate the countries or areas covered in the essays.

- For each viewpoint, an **introduction** that contains notes about the author and source of the viewpoint explains why material from the specific country is being presented, summarizes the main points of the viewpoint, and offers three **guided reading questions** to aid in understanding and comprehension.

- **For further discussion** questions that promote critical thinking by asking the reader to compare and contrast aspects of the viewpoints or draw conclusions about perspectives and arguments.

- A worldwide list of **organizations to contact** for readers seeking additional information.

- A **periodical bibliography** for each chapter and a **bibliography of books** on the volume topic to aid in further research.

- A comprehensive **subject index** to offer access to people, places, events, and subjects cited in the text, with the countries covered in the viewpoints highlighted.

Global Viewpoints is designed for a broad spectrum of readers who want to learn more about current events, history, political science, government, international relations, economics, environmental science, world cultures, and sociology—students doing research for class assignments or debates, teachers and faculty seeking to supplement course materials, and others wanting to understand current issues better. By presenting how people in various countries perceive the root causes, current consequences, and proposed solutions to worldwide challenges, *Global Viewpoints* volumes offer readers opportunities to enhance their global awareness and their knowledge of cultures worldwide.

Introduction

"We used to be a source of fuel; we are increasingly becoming a sink. These supplies of foreign liquid fuel are no doubt vital to our industry, but our ever-increasing dependence upon them ought to arouse serious and timely reflection."

—Winston Churchill, speaking in 1928

On August 21, 2009, an oil and gas platform in the Timor Sea off the western coast of Australia began to leak oil, gas, and condensate. The leak was located 31.6 miles below the ocean floor. The company, PTTEP Australasia, tried several times to plug the leak; on the fifth attempt, a damaging fire broke out, engulfing the entire platform and the drilling rig above it. The fire raged for days, until the company was able to pump heavy mud and brine down into the relief well, which plugged the leak and put out the fire. By that time, oil had been leaking into the Timor Sea unchecked for ten weeks.

Assessing the damage, Australian officials estimated that approximately three thousand barrels of oil leaked a day, making it one of the worst oil spills in the country's history. Environmental groups cited satellite photos, which showed the oil spill spread across more than nine thousand square miles, and estimated that nearly 9 million gallons leaked into the Timor Sea. The public was shocked—the 1989 *Exxon Valdez* disaster in Alaska leaked 11 million gallons into Prince William Sound. This was certainly a serious environmental disaster that spelled the death of thousands of whales, dolphins, turtles, fish, and sea birds that flocked to the waters of the western Australia coast. Although cleanup efforts were launched right away, environmentalists were pessimistic about the efforts. "There's no cleanup technology available on earth to clean up a spill that big," said Richard Charter of the animal conservation group, Defenders of Wildlife.

The Timor Sea spill was just the latest in a line of environmental disasters caused by the drilling for or transportation of oil. Yet despite the gigantic risks to not only oceans and marine wildlife, but also fishing and tourism industries that flourish along many coastlines in the world, nations are more frequently allowing oil companies to explore and develop oil wells in protected, isolated, or environmentally sensitive areas—even when it is not clear what the ultimate payoff will be in oil production. The reason for these gambles is the prospect of peak oil.

Peak oil is defined as the point when the maximum rate of global oil production is reached. After peak oil is achieved, the rate of production declines. For an oil field, peak oil is the peak of oil production; once decline starts, it progresses precipitously until the field is depleted. Peak oil also refers to the global rate of petroleum production.

A heated debate rages as to the point of global peak oil production. Optimistic projections predict that global decline will begin around 2020. Pessimistic projects argue that peak oil has already passed, or will occur shortly. In other words, many experts believe that we have already reached the earth's maximum oil production and are now on a slow, but inexorable, decline.

Evidence seems to support the idea that the world's oil supply is not inexhaustible and that we are seeing the limits of years of voracious consumption of oil. According to recent International Energy Agency reports, global oil-production growth trends were flat from 2005 to 2008. Of the largest and most productive oil fields in the world, at least nine have passed peak oil and are currently in decline. In April 2006, a spokesman from Saudi Aramco, the state-owned national oil company of Saudi Arabia, disclosed that the country's oil fields are declining at a significant rate. Even Saudi Arabia's largest field, which is the largest oil field in the world, Ghawar, is considered to be in significant decline. Ghawar has accounted for approximately half of Saudi Arabia's oil production since the mid-1950s.

With the prospect of peak oil looming, or perhaps past, and the threat of a global downturn in oil production, oil companies have been looking far and wide for new regions to explore and develop oil sources. One action oil companies are taking is pursuing and obtaining leases in areas once thought too isolated, difficult, or environmentally sensitive. For example, the U.S. Department of the Interior gave approval for Shell to drill exploration wells in the notoriously difficult Beaufort Sea, an area off the north coast of Alaska and bordering the Arctic Ocean. It is known for being virtually untouched by man and home to endangered polar bears, whales, and numerous Arctic animals. Environmentalists charge that an oil spill in this isolated area would be catastrophic.

Further examples of this trend are the Dreki, or dragon zone, an isolated region off the northeast coast of Iceland, and the Lofoten Islands, off the coast of Norway. Several countries are also jockeying to claim the untapped oil potential of the Arctic, as wide swaths of once frozen sea are now accessible because of global warming.

Conflicts between governments, oil companies, and environmental groups are inevitable as the world's oil fields reach peak oil and the supply of oil continues to decline, leaving oil companies to explore and develop oil resources in more difficult and environmentally sensitive areas. Energy companies are opting to explore and develop smaller wells in more complicated and trying regions in order to fulfill the insatiable global demand for petroleum.

As well as new regions, energy companies are exploring new sources of oil. One key source is the development of oil sands, also known as tar sands. These sands are a combination of sand or clay, water, and bitumen, which is a type of petroleum. Technological advances have allowed oil companies to profitably extract petroleum. Large oil sands reserves are found in western Canada and Venezuela.

The authors of the viewpoints presented in *Global Viewpoints: Oil* discuss some of the key issues of global concern: oil and the economy, oil and the environment, oil and politics, and drilling for new sources of oil. The information provided in this volume will provide insight into the recurring conflict between environmentalists, who want to protect pristine areas and endangered wildlife, and energy company officials, who want to find new sources of oil to continue providing fuel for countries and consumers for years to come.

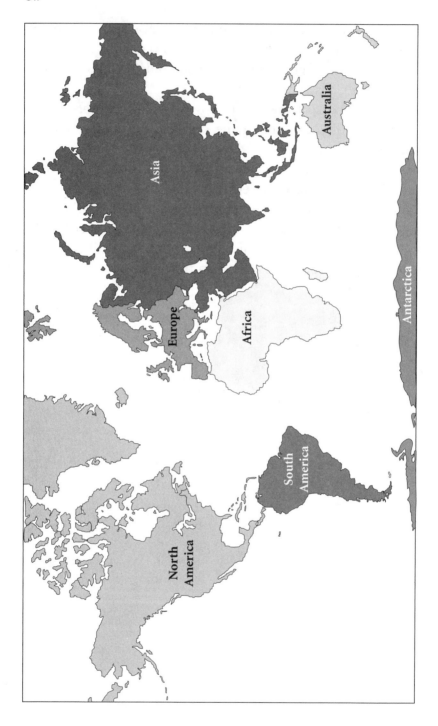

GLOBAL VIEWPOINTS

CHAPTER 1

Oil and the Economy

The Global Oil Outlook: An Overview

International Energy Agency

The International Energy Agency (IEA) is an intergovernmental organization that functions as an energy policy advisor to member countries. In the following viewpoint excerpted from its yearly report on the global energy outlook, the agency offers a thorough analysis of the current state of global oil supplies and outlines the energy challenges facing the world in the next few decades. The IEA also advocates long-term cooperation between nations in order to implement a clear, effective program to curb greenhouse gas emissions to alleviate climate change.

As you read, consider the following questions:

1. How many degrees Celsius does the IEA believe the global temperature will rise as a result of energy-related emissions of greenhouse gases, especially carbon dioxide?
2. According to IEA projections, by what percentage will world primary energy demand grow per year?
3. What percentage of the world's primary energy mix will fossil fuels account for in 2030, according to IEA estimates?

International Energy Agency, "Executive Summary," *World Energy Outlook 2009*, 75739 Paris Cedex 15: International Energy Agency (IEA), 2009, pp. 3–9. Copyright © OECD/IEA, 2009. Reproduced by permission.

The past 12 months have seen enormous upheavals in energy markets around the world, yet the challenges of transforming the global energy system remain urgent and daunting. The global financial crisis and ensuing recession have had a dramatic impact on the outlook for energy markets, particularly in the next few years. World energy demand in aggregate has already plunged with the economic contraction; how quickly it rebounds depends largely on how quickly the global economy recovers. Countries have responded to the threat of economic meltdown as a result of the financial crisis with prompt and coordinated fiscal and monetary stimuli on an unprecedented scale. In many cases, stimulus packages have included measures to promote clean energy with the aim of tackling an even bigger, and just as real, long-term threat—that of disastrous climate change.

How we rise to that challenge will have far-reaching consequences for energy markets. As the leading source of greenhouse gas emissions, energy is at the heart of the problem and so must be integral to the solution. The time to act has arrived: the 15th Conference of the Parties (COP 15) to the United Nations Framework Convention on Climate Change (UNFCCC) in Copenhagen (December 2009) presents a decisive opportunity to negotiate a successor treaty to the Kyoto Protocol—one that puts the world on to a truly sustainable energy path. The *World Energy Outlook* 2009 (WEO-2009) quantifies the challenge and shows what is required to overcome it.

The scale and breadth of the energy challenge is enormous—far greater than many people realise. But it can and must be met. The recession, by curbing the growth in greenhouse gas emissions, has made the task of transforming the energy sector easier by giving us an unprecedented, yet relatively narrow, window of opportunity to take action to concentrate investment on low-carbon technology. Energy-related carbon dioxide (CO_2) emissions in 2009 will be well below what they would have been had the recession not occurred. But this saving will count for nothing if a robust deal is not reached in Copenhagen—and emissions resume their upward path.

Households and businesses are largely responsible for making the required investments, but governments hold the key to changing the mix of energy investment. The policy and regulatory frameworks established at national and international levels will determine whether investment and consumption decisions are steered towards low-carbon options. Accordingly, this outlook presents the results of two scenarios: a *Reference Scenario*, which provides a baseline picture of how global energy markets would evolve if governments make no changes to their existing policies and measures; and a *450 Scenario*, which depicts a world in which collective policy action is taken to limit the long-term concentration of greenhouse gases in the atmosphere to 450 parts per million of CO_2-equivalent (ppm CO_2-eq), an objective that is gaining widespread support around the world.

The Financial Crisis Brings a Temporary Reprieve from Rising Fossil Energy Use

Global energy use is set to fall in 2009—for the first time since 1981 on any significant scale—as a result of the financial and economic crisis; but, on current policies, it would quickly resume its long-term upward trend once economic recovery is underway. In our Reference Scenario, world primary energy demand is projected to increase by 1.5% per year between 2007 and 2030, from just over 12000 million tonnes of oil equivalent (Mtoe) to 16800 Mtoe—an overall increase of 40%. Developing Asian countries are the main drivers of this growth, followed by the Middle East. Projected demand growth is slower than in WEO-2008 [*World Energy Outlook* 2008], reflecting mainly the impact of the crisis in the early part of the projection period, as well as of new government policies introduced during the past year. On average, demand declines marginally in 2007–2010, as a result of a sharp drop in 2009—preliminary data point to a fall in that year of up to 2%. Demand growth rebounds thereafter, averaging 2.5% per year in 2010–2015. The pace of demand growth slackens progressively after 2015, as emerging economies mature and global population growth slows.

Fossil fuels remain the dominant sources of primary energy worldwide in the Reference Scenario, accounting for more than three-quarters of the overall increase in energy use between 2007 and 2030. In absolute terms, coal sees by far the biggest increase in demand over the projection period, followed by gas and oil. Yet oil remains the single largest fuel in the primary fuel mix in 2030, even though its share drops, from 34% now to 30%. Oil demand (excluding biofuels) is projected to grow by 1% per year on average over the projection period, from 85 million barrels per day in 2008 to 105 mb/d [millions of barrels per day] in 2030. All the growth comes from non-OECD [Organisation for Economic Co-operation and Development] countries: OECD demand actually falls. The transport sector accounts for 97% of the increase in oil use. As conventional oil production in countries not belonging to the Organization of the Petroleum Exporting Countries (OPEC) peaks around 2010, most of the increase in output would need to come from OPEC countries, which hold the bulk of remaining recoverable conventional oil resources.

The main driver of demand for coal and gas is the inexorable growth in energy needs for power generation. World electricity demand is projected to grow at an annual rate of 2.5% to 2030. Over 80% of the growth takes place in non-OECD countries. Globally, additions to power-generation capacity total 4800 gigawatts (GW) by 2030—almost five times the existing capacity of the United States. The largest additions (around 28% of the total) occur in China. Coal remains the backbone fuel of the power sector, its share of the global generation mix rising by three percentage points to 44% in 2030. Nuclear power output grows in all major regions bar Europe, but its share in total generation falls.

The use of non-hydro modern renewable energy technologies (including wind, solar, geothermal, tide and wave energy, and bio-energy) sees the fastest rate of increase in the Reference Scenario. Most of the increase is in power generation: The share of non-hydro renewables in total power output rises from 2.5% in 2007 to 8.6% in 2030, with wind power seeing the biggest absolute increase. The consumption of biofuels for transport also rises strongly. The share of hydropower, by contrast, drops from 16% to 14%.

"Fossil fuels remain the dominant sources of primary energy worldwide in the Reference Scenario, accounting for more than three-quarters of the overall increase in energy use between 2007 and 2030."

Falling Energy Investment Will Have Far-Reaching Consequences

Energy investment worldwide has plunged over the past year in the face of a tougher financing environment, weakening final demand for energy and lower cash flow. All these factors stem from the financial and economic crisis. Energy companies are drilling fewer oil and gas wells, and cutting back spending on refineries, pipelines and power stations. Many ongoing projects have been slowed and a number of planned projects have been postponed or cancelled. Businesses and households are spending less on new, more efficient energy-using appliances, equipment and vehicles, with important knock-on effects for the efficiency of energy use in the long term.

In the oil and gas sector, most companies have announced cutbacks in capital spending, as well as project delays and cancellations, mainly as a result of lower cash flow. We estimate that global upstream oil and gas investment budgets for 2009 have been cut by around 19% compared with 2008—a reduction of over $90 billion. Oil sands projects in Canada account for the bulk of the suspended oil capacity. Power sector investment is also being severely affected by financing difficulties, as well as by weak demand, which is reducing the immediate need for new capacity additions. In late 2008 and early 2009, investment in renewables fell proportionately more than that in other types of generating capacity; for 2009 as a whole, it could drop by close to one-fifth. Without the stimulus provided by government fiscal packages, renewables investment would have fallen by almost 30%.

Falling energy investment will have far-reaching and, depending on how governments respond, potentially serious consequences for energy security, climate change and energy poverty. Any prolonged downturn in investment threatens to constrain capacity growth in the medium term, particularly for long lead-time projects, eventually risking a shortfall in supply. This could lead to a renewed surge in prices a few years down the line, when demand is likely to be recovering, and become a constraint on global economic growth. These concerns are most acute for oil and electricity supplies. Any such shortfalls could, in turn, undermine the sustainability of the economic recovery. Weaker fossil fuel prices are also undermining the attractiveness of investments in clean energy technology (though recent government moves to encourage such investment, as part of their economic stimulus packages, are helping to counter this effect). Cutbacks in energy-infrastructure investments also threaten to impede access by poor households to electricity and other forms of modern energy.

The financial crisis has cast a shadow over whether all the energy investment needed to meet growing energy needs can be mobilised. The capital required to meet projected energy demand through to 2030 in the Reference Scenario is huge, amounting in cumulative terms to $26 trillion (in year 2008 dollars)—equal to $1.1 trillion (or 1.4% of global gross domestic product [GDP]) per year on average. The power sector requires 53% of total investment. Over half of all energy investment worldwide is needed in developing countries, where demand and production are projected to increase fastest. With little prospect of a quick return to the days of cheap and easy credit, financing energy investment will, in most cases, be more difficult and costly in the medium term than it was before the crisis took hold.

Current Policies Put Us on an Alarming Fossil-Energy Path

Continuing on today's energy path, without any change in government policy, would mean rapidly increasing dependence on fossil fuels, with alarming consequences for climate change and energy security. The Reference Scenario sees a continued rapid rise in energy-related CO_2 emissions through to 2030, resulting from increased global demand for fossil energy. Having already increased from 20.9 gigatonnes (Gt) in 1990 to 28.8 Gt in 2007, CO_2 emissions are projected to reach 34.5 Gt in 2020 and 40.2 Gt in 2030—an average rate of growth of 1.5% per year over the full projection period. In 2020 global emissions are 1.9 Gt or 5% lower than in the Reference Scenario of WEO-2008. The economic crisis and resulting lower fossil energy demand growth account for three-quarters of this improvement, while government stimulus spending to promote low-carbon investments and other new energy and climate policies account for the remainder. Preliminary data suggest that global energy-related emissions of CO_2 may *decline* in 2009—possibly by around 3%—although they are expected to resume an upward trajectory from 2010.

Non-OECD countries account for all of the projected growth in energy-related CO_2 emissions to 2030. Three-

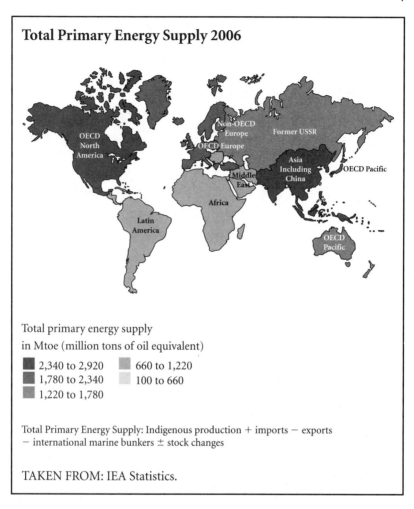

Total Primary Energy Supply 2006

Total primary energy supply
in Mtoe (million tons of oil equivalent)

- 2,340 to 2,920
- 1,780 to 2,340
- 1,220 to 1,780
- 660 to 1,220
- 100 to 660

Total Primary Energy Supply: Indigenous production + imports − exports
− international marine bunkers ± stock changes

TAKEN FROM: IEA Statistics.

quarters of the 11-Gt increase comes from China (where emissions rise by 6 Gt), India (2 Gt) and the Middle East (1 Gt). OECD emissions are projected to fall slightly, due to a slowdown in energy demand (resulting from the crisis in the near term and from big improvements in energy efficiency in the longer term) and the increased reliance on nuclear power and renewables, in large part due to the policies already adopted to mitigate climate change and enhance energy security. By contrast, all major non-OECD countries see their emissions rise. However, while non-OECD countries today account for

52% of the world's annual emissions of energy-related CO_2, they are responsible for only 42% of the world's cumulative emissions since 1890.

These trends would lead to a rapid increase in the concentration of greenhouse gases in the atmosphere. The rate of growth of fossil energy consumption projected in the Reference Scenario takes us inexorably towards a long-term concentration of greenhouse gases in the atmosphere in excess of 1000 ppm CO_2-eq. The CO_2 concentration implied by the Reference Scenario would result in the global average temperature rising by up to 6°C. This would lead almost certainly to massive climatic change and irreparable damage to the planet.

The Reference Scenario trends also heighten concerns about the security of energy supplies. While the OECD imports less oil in 2030 than today in the Reference Scenario, some non-OECD countries, notably China and India, see big increases in their imports. Most gas-importing regions, including Europe and developing Asia, also see their net imports rise. The Reference Scenario projections imply an increasingly high level of spending on energy imports, representing a major economic burden for importers. Oil prices are assumed to fall from the 2008 level of $97 per barrel to around $60 per barrel in 2009 (roughly the level of mid-2009), but then rebound with the economic recovery to reach $100 per barrel by 2020 and $115 per barrel by 2030 (in year 2008 dollars). As a result, OECD countries as a group are projected to spend on average close to 2% of their GDP on oil and gas imports to 2030. The burden is even higher in most importing non-OECD countries. On a country basis, China overtakes the United States soon after 2025 to become the world's biggest spender on oil and gas imports (in monetary terms) while India's spending on oil and gas imports surpasses that of Japan soon after 2020 to become the world's third-largest importer. The increasing concentration of the world's remaining conventional oil and gas reserves in a small group of countries, including Russia and resource-rich Middle East countries, would increase their market power and ability to influence prices.

Expanding access to modern energy for the world's poor remains a pressing matter. We estimate that 1.5 billion people still lack access to electricity—well over one-fifth of the world's population. Some 85% of those people live in rural areas, mainly in sub-Saharan Africa and South Asia. In the Reference Scenario, the total number drops by only around 200 million by 2030, though the number actually increases in Africa. Expanding access to modern energy is a necessary condition for human development. With appropriate policies, universal electricity access could be achieved with additional annual investment worldwide of $35 billion (in year 2008 dollars) through to 2030, or just 6% of the power-sector investment projected in the Reference Scenario. The accompanying increase in primary energy demand and CO_2 emissions would be very modest.

Limiting Temperature Rise to 2°C Requires a Low-Carbon Energy Revolution

Although opinion is mixed on what might be considered a sustainable, long-term level of annual CO_2 emissions for the energy sector, a consensus on the need to limit the global temperature increase to 2°C is emerging. To limit to 50% the probability of a global average temperature increase in excess of 2°C, the concentration of greenhouse gases in the atmosphere would need to be stabilised at a level around 450 ppm CO_2-eq. We show how this objective can be achieved in the 450 Scenario, through radical and coordinated policy action across all regions. In this scenario, global energy-related CO_2 emissions peak at 30.9 Gt just before 2020 and decline thereafter to 26.4 Gt in 2030—2.4 Gt below the 2007 level and 13.8 Gt below that in the Reference Scenario. These reductions result from a plausible combination of policy instruments—notably carbon markets, sectoral agreements and national policies and measures—tailored to the circumstances of specific sectors and groups of countries. Only by taking advantage of mitigation potential in all sectors and regions can the necessary emission reductions be achieved. OECD+ countries (a group that includes the OECD and non-OECD EU countries) are assumed to take on national emission-reduction commitments from 2013. All other countries are assumed to adopt domestic policies and measures, and to generate and sell emissions credits. After 2020, commitments are extended to other major economies—a group comprising China, Russia, Brazil, South Africa and the Middle East.

The reductions in energy-related CO_2 emissions required in the 450 Scenario (relative to the Reference Scenario) by 2020—just a decade away—are formidable, but the financial crisis offers what may be a unique opportunity to take the necessary steps as the political mood shifts. At 30.7 Gt, emissions in 2020 in the 450 Scenario are 3.8 Gt lower than in the Reference Scenario. In non-OECD countries, national policies currently under consideration, along with sectoral approaches in transport and industry, yield 1.6 Gt of emission abatement. But this abatement will not happen in the absence of an appropriate international framework. The challenge for international negotiators is to find instruments that will give the right level of additional incentive to ensure that the necessary measures are implemented. With national policies, China alone accounts for 1 Gt of emissions reductions in the 450 Scenario, placing the country at the forefront of global efforts to combat climate change. The remaining reductions in 2010 are delivered by OECD+ countries through an emissions cap in the power and industry sectors, domestic policies, and by financing, through the carbon market, additional abatement in non-OECD countries. In 2010, the OECD+ carbon price reaches $50 per tonne of CO_2. The financial and economic crisis has temporarily slowed the lock-in of high-carbon energy technologies. With the prospect of demand picking up over the next few years, it is crucial to put in place an agreement providing clear economic signals to encourage the deployment of low-carbon technologies.

With a new international climate policy agreement, a comprehensive and rapid transformation in the way we produce, transport and use energy—a veritable low-carbon revolution—could put the world on to this 450-ppm trajectory. Energy needs to be used more efficiently and the carbon content of the energy we consume must be reduced, by switching to low—or zero—carbon sources. In the 450 Scenario, primary energy demand grows by 20% between 2007 and 2030. This corresponds to an average annual growth rate of 0.8%, compared with 1.5% in the Reference Scenario. Increased energy efficiency in buildings and industry reduces the demand for electricity and, to a lesser extent, fossil fuels. The average emissions intensity of new cars is reduced by more than half, cutting oil needs. The share of non-fossil fuels in the overall primary energy mix increases from 19% in 2007 to 32% in 2030, when CO_2 emissions per unit of GDP are less than half their 2007 level. Yet, with the exception of coal, demand for all fuels is higher in 2030 than in 2007, and fossil fuels remain the dominant energy sources in 2030.

Energy Efficiency Offers Biggest Scope for Cutting Emissions

End-use efficiency is the largest contributor to CO_2 emissions abatement in 2030, accounting for more than half of total savings in the 450 Scenario, compared with the Reference Scenario. Energy-efficiency investments in buildings, industry and transport usually have short payback periods and negative net abatement costs, as the fuel-cost savings over the lifetime of the capital stock often outweigh the additional capital cost of the efficiency measure, even when future savings are discounted. Decarbonisation of the power sector also plays a central role in reducing emissions. Power generation accounts for more than two-thirds of the savings in the 450 Scenario (of which 40% results from lower electricity demand). There is a big shift in the mix of fuels and technologies in power generation: Coal-based generation is reduced by half, compared with the Reference Scenario in 2030, while nuclear power and renewables make much bigger contributions. The United States and China together contribute about half of the reduction in global power-sector emissions. Carbon capture and storage (CCS) in the power sector and in industry represents 10% of total emissions savings in 2030, relative to the Reference Scenario.

Measures in the transport sector to improve fuel economy, expand biofuels and promote the uptake of new vehicle technologies—notably hybrid and electric vehicles—lead to a big reduction in oil demand. By 2030, transport demand for oil is cut by 12 mb/d, equal to more than 70% of all the oil savings in the 450 Scenario. Road transport accounts for the vast majority of these transport-related oil savings. A dramatic shift in car sales occurs by 2030, conventional internal combustion engines represent only about 40% of sales, down from more than 90% in the Reference Scenario, as hybrids take up 30% of sales and plug-in hybrids and electric vehicles account for the remainder. Efficiency improvements in new aircraft and the use of biofuels in aviation save 1.6 mb/d of oil demand by 2030. . . .

German Concern Over Oil Prices Threatens European Prosperity

Der Spiegel

Der Spiegel is a prominent German weekly magazine and one of Europe's most widely read publications. In the following viewpoint, Spiegel's staff reports that German citizens have been hit with significant increases in oil, electricity, and natural gas prices. Consumer anxiety over these rising prices and the flat German economy has threatened the coalition government's climate package and has caused a rift among the ruling parties.

As you read, consider the following questions:

1. According to *Der Spiegel*, heating and electricity bills now account for what percentage of total housing costs for the average German citizen?
2. How much do experts predict oil prices could rise by the end of 2009 in Germany, according to the viewpoint?
3. Since 2000, how much has the price of natural gas increased for German consumers, according to the viewpoint?

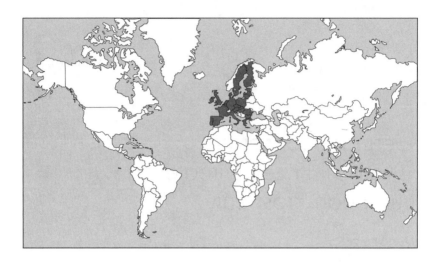

Vitali Minakow has already changed many of his habits to cope with the daily frustration at the gas pump. He takes fewer vacations, rides his bike to work and reaches for the phone instead of meeting friends in person. "I used to just fill the tank up and drive off," says Minakow, a forklift driver from the western German city of Osnabrück. "But that just doesn't work anymore."

Minakow feels trapped. No matter what he gives up, gas prices still squeeze more and more from his wallet. "My salary has stayed the same for years," he says, "but gas just keeps getting more and more expensive."

Germans are experiencing a particularly unpleasant kind of energy crisis. They conserve electricity and gas where they can, but costs for heating the house, driving, cooking and taking a morning shower are making a bigger and bigger dent in the household budget. Since the price of a barrel of oil first broke the $135 mark last week [May 2008], filling the gas tank of a Volkswagen Golf now costs more than €80 ($125).

A commuter who makes the daily, 65-kilometer (40-mile) commute between the northern cities of Lübeck and Hamburg will fork out an additional €500 ($778) this year just for gas. Heating and electricity bills have also recently climbed to that point that they now account for 40 percent of total housing costs. If the trend continues, utility costs will become a "second rent," complains Franz-Georg Rips, president of the German national tenants association.

"Germans are experiencing a particularly unpleasant kind of energy crisis."

What is really worrying Germans, though, is the fear that this "oil price madness," as Germany's mass-circulation daily *Bild* calls it, could become a permanent condition. In the past, energy prices would shoot up but then drop again, and people didn't necessarily feel poorer. Now, though, it seems that Germans' energy bills will continue to grow faster than their incomes and that the price hike for oil, natural gas, gasoline and electricity will begin threatening economic well-being.

For economists and consumers alike, all previous calculations are now out the window. Whereas earlier a majority of experts predicted robust growth for 2008, they now see an economy in serious danger.

A Political Conundrum

In Berlin, too, views are changing. The same politicians who have always made fighting global warming their top priority are now outdoing themselves with suggestions that will take the pressure off consumers. Environment Minister Sigmar Gabriel wants relief for low-income commuters. Erwin Huber, leader of the Christian Social Union (CSU)—the Bavarian sister party of the conservative Christian Democratic Union (CDU)—advocates general tax cuts. Even environmental expert Bärbel Höhn of the Greens—for whom energy prices up to now couldn't rise fast enough—is suddenly calling for limits, preferably through the introduction of "red cards for speculators."

Last week witnessed the first victim of this new mood about the economy: the grand coalition's climate package. The set of measures to limit CO_2 emissions was supposed to be passed in the cabinet on Tuesday [May 20, 2008]. But the grand coalition's partners, the center-left Social Democratic Party (SPD) and the CDU, couldn't agree on how many additional costs could still be imposed on their constituents in the face of rising energy costs. Once again, the program was put off.

This new oil and energy crisis is bringing up plenty of questions, and not just for the two main political parties. How can consumers absorb the costs? How much climate protection can be imposed on consumers if the costs of oil, natural gas, gasoline, and electricity are also rising? Should energy taxes be lowered or increased?

These questions are urgent. Energy prices are already rising higher, driven by three simultaneous factors: the growing hunger for raw materials in emerging economies such as China and India; the greed of speculators; and additional governmental charges, including those related to climate protection. According to experts' predictions, the future holds more price increases—and the change will be especially drastic for drivers.

Pain, Not Just at the Pump

Hardly a day goes by without the Chicago Board of Trade registering a new record price for a barrel of oil. And, every day, consumers feel the consequence of this most immediately at the gas pump. Last week, prices for super gasoline and diesel in Germany broke the €1.50 per liter barrier—and there is no end in sight. Experts predict that, by the end of 2009, oil prices could rise to $200 (€129) a barrel. On Wednesday, Airbus CEO Thomas Enders warned that, were that to happen, Germany's aircraft industry would "collapse."

The same development can be seen with the fuel most Germans use to heat their homes. Since 2000, the price of natural gas has shot up around 75 percent and had dramatic consequences for consumers. In many cases, since the turn of the millennium, the gas bill for a three-person household has increased by several hundred euros per year.

"Hardly a day goes by without the Chicago Board of Trade registering a new record price for a barrel of oil."

And the current year will bring additional changes, according to internal calculations of Düsseldorf-based energy provider E.ON, and changes that the industry has never seen. In fact, the company sees a "need to adjust gas prices"—to use the euphemistic corporate jargon—by up to 25 percent.

There is no conclusive decision yet as to exactly when the price increase will be announced and whether it would be better to make this massive jump in one step or two. But it is certain that other companies will follow E.ON, the market leader, if they are not already independently planning similar price increases.

The average three-person household would then have to pay around €400 ($622) more for natural gas than it does today. From around their current €1,600 value, heating bills would jump to as high as €2,000. Even energy providers themselves believe that this would reach a magnitude that many households would find very difficult or impossible to bear. In recent years, public utilities have already reported a growing trend of outstanding debts, as more and more customers are unable to pay their bills.

Likewise, for electricity prices, no relief is in sight for consumers or the industry, and the already record prices will continue to soar.

Reduced Power Generation

The reason behind this is not just the fact that competition on the energy market has been slow in emerging or the enormous market power of Germany's four dominant energy suppliers. Dramatic changes in the power-generation industry have also had an effect on prices. The decision to abandon nuclear power made by the former red-green ruling coalition of the Social Democrats and the Greens means that, in the coming years, almost a quarter of Germany's power-generating capacity will disappear. How that lost capacity will be replaced remains an open question.

Throughout the country, there is considerable resistance to new, modern coal plants. Even completely outdated power plants are no longer replaced by the companies that run them because climate-minded citizens' initiatives campaign so intensely against new billion-euro construction projects.

The German Energy Agency recently projected the consequences of this trend and reports that Germany is not only in danger of facing a shortage in the power supply, but also that increasingly scarce capacity will force substantial price increases.

Renewable energy sources, such as water, wind and solar power, will hardly be able to fill these energy gaps looming in the foreseeable future. Even the federal government's plan to secure around 30 percent of the power supply from such sources by the year 2020 is extremely ambitious—and expensive.

In order to reach that goal, the government has been giving generous subsidies to producers of solar power, wind energy and biomass. These energy producers brought in around €7.7 billion ($12 billion) last year on top of what they collected from customers' electricity bills, and this amount will see annual increases that will reach around €12.5 billion ($19.5 billion) by 2013. Subsidies for alternative energy currently cost the average German household around €30 ($47) annually and, in eight years, it will be almost twice as much.

The Role of CO_2 Reduction

There is another factor that may start driving costs up for industry and consumers in the foreseeable future. Since the beginning of 2008, the government has been auctioning off pollution rights for carbon dioxide emissions. At first, only 10 percent of certificates will exchange hands in this way each year.

But that's just the beginning. As the European Commission imagines it, starting in 2013, all emissions rights for energy corporations will be sold by auction and subsequently traded like gold or stocks. And because considerably fewer certificates will be issued than there will be CO_2 emitted in Europe, there is an incentive for companies to implement clean technology or to shut down old facilities early.

"It's no wonder that economic researchers are worried about the predicted energy conservation shock."

In fact, according to a study by the German Association of Industrial Energy and Power Management (VIK), energy providers will have to pay the government between €9 billion and €14 billion ($14 billion and $21.8 billion) every year from 2013 to 2020 for these certificates. Companies will largely be able to pass these costs on to consumers, and electricity costs are likely to climb drastically.

Under these circumstances, it's no wonder that economic researchers are worried about the predicted energy conservation shock. According to the calculations of Claudia Kemfert, energy expert at the Berlin-based German Institute for Economic Research, Germans will spend around €90 billion ($140

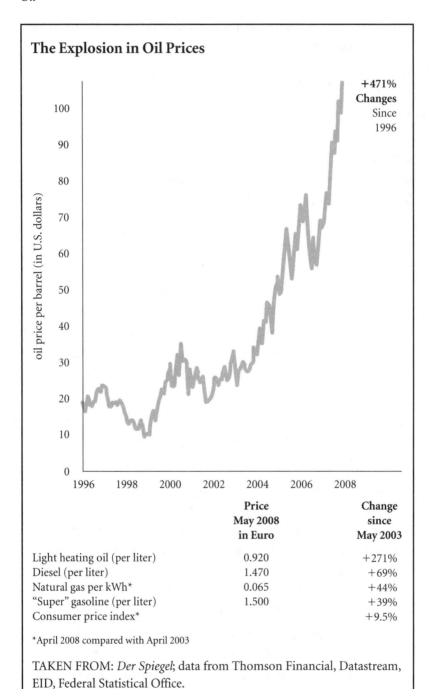

The Explosion in Oil Prices

+471%
Changes
Since
1996

oil price per barrel (in U.S. dollars)

	Price May 2008 in Euro	Change since May 2003
Light heating oil (per liter)	0.920	+271%
Diesel (per liter)	1.470	+69%
Natural gas per kWh*	0.065	+44%
"Super" gasoline (per liter)	1.500	+39%
Consumer price index*		+9.5%

*April 2008 compared with April 2003

TAKEN FROM: *Der Spiegel*; data from Thomson Financial, Datastream, EID, Federal Statistical Office.

billion) this year on coal, oil and natural gas. That's €15 billion ($23.4 billion), or 20 percent, more than they did last year.

"That's a significant cost burden for the German economy," says Kemfert. And, since the additional expenditures of businesses and households for energy mean fewer funds left over to cover other costs, it's also a danger to the economy. Businesses invest less in new machinery, and consumers no longer go out to restaurants and cinemas or refrain from buying new cars, all of which are factors that slow economic growth.

Economists had actually hoped that private consumption would boom this year, and that it would assume the role of the economy's main driving force. For now, though, nothing has come of that, and consumer demand is stagnant.

The Environmental Hit

As they look to the future—and even though the German economy showed an impressive 1.5 percent growth rate in the first quarter [of 2008]—many economic experts are already considerably more pessimistic. The fear now is that this could simply result in the coming crash being all the more severe.

Moreover, according to the latest predictions, the currently high energy prices could seriously reduce this year's rate of growth. That the economy suffers when energy prices rise is hardly surprising. But there could be a second victim of the increasing costs in Germany: the environment.

German Chancellor Angela Merkel had planned to make this week the tentative high point of her environment strategy. Before presenting herself to the world as nature's protector on Wednesday at the UN Convention on Biological Diversity in Bonn, Merkel wanted to finalize her climate-policy masterpiece in the cabinet. The last outstanding decisions were supposed to be resolved, such as how by 2020 Germans would emit 40 percent less carbon dioxide than they did in 1990.

The package of measures is called "Meseberg 2" after the federal government's guesthouse near Berlin. It was there, last summer, that the grand coalition last demonstrated something like a capacity for action.

Now the whole plan—from energy conservation and heating cost regulations to environmental taxation of automobiles—threatens to collapse around Merkel.

A Wedge in the Coalition

Since energy prices started their rapid rise, Merkel's party has developed a phobia of anything that might carry a whiff of further costs to the electorate. "We judge every measure first and foremost in terms of costs for the consumer," says Katherina Reiche, the deputy chairwoman of the CDU's parliamentary group, in describing the party's new line. Using this battle cry, CDU members of Parliament are fighting to cut the conservation requirements in the package as much as possible.

Environment Minister Gabriel's behavior is just as inconsistent. On the one hand, he urges that the Meseberg package be waved through without any cuts. On the other, he advocates for commuter tax relief calculated to help owners of older, less fuel-efficient cars, a demographic he evidently assumes to include a high number of voters for his party, the SPD.

"Germany ultimately wants to move away from oil, and the increase in prices is sending the right signal."

The CDU-SPD coalition is hopelessly at odds with itself, failing to make a decision on stricter regulations for energy conservation or to provide incentives for environmentally friendly cars and trucks. Last week the coalition was unable to reach an expected agreement on a reform of the automobile tax, and the remaining points of the Meseberg package were postponed once again. Now more than ever, it is unclear how the government plans to reach its loudly proclaimed goal of cutting CO_2 emissions by a further 20 percent over the next 12 years.

A Silver Lining?

Yet, at the same time, experts actually see in the rising energy prices of the last months a chance to bring the economy and the environment even closer together. It would be wrong, they argue, to try to counteract the hike in oil and natural gas prices by reducing the petroleum tax or environmental taxes. According to their reasoning, Germany ultimately wants to move away from oil, and the increase in prices is sending the right signal.

In their opinion, the right reaction to an increasing scarcity of resources would be to implement the government's climate-protection measures more efficiently than is currently being done. More funds need to be allocated to modernizing antiquated power plants, they argue, and fewer to questionable subsidies for the expensive solar power industry.

Nevertheless, it appears that the CDU and SPD can no longer agree on a rational energy and climate policy. Instead, both sides prefer to sharpen their battle rhetoric. For example, a high-ranking employee at Gabriel's Environment Ministry says: "The CDU and CSU sit there like the Russians during the Cold War and answer everything with 'nyet ['no'].'"

Venezuela's Economy Is Shaped by Oil Prices

Mark Weisbrot

Mark Weisbrot is the codirector of the Center for Economic and Policy Research and a frequent commentator on economic issues. In the following essay, he explores the extent to which Venezuela's economy is tied to oil prices. Weisbrot concludes that although there is a strong connection, the Venezuelan economy has some flexibility to make up for flat oil prices and the global economic slowdown.

As you read, consider the following questions:

1. How much does the author say the Venezuelan economy has grown since the second quarter of 2003?
2. In what sector has the bulk of this growth occurred, according to Weisbrot?
3. Petroleum makes up what percentage of Venezuela's exports, according to the viewpoint?

The Venezuelan economy has grown more than 94 percent since the current expansion began in the second quarter of 2003. The overwhelming bulk of this growth has been in the non-oil sector. Throughout most of these five and a half years of unprecedented growth, the economy has often been

Mark Weisbrot, "Oil Prices and Venezuela's Economy," Center for Economic and Policy Research, November 21, 2008. Reproduced by permission of the author. www.cepr.net.

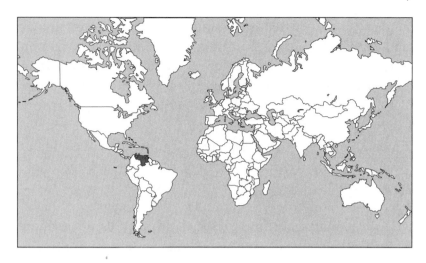

characterized as an "oil boom about to go bust," and predictions of collapse have been commonplace and often repeated. These have become more numerous of late since oil prices have fallen nearly 50 percent from a peak of over $130 in July [2008] to their current $64.48 per barrel. The current financial crisis, worldwide stock market collapse, and recession in the United States, Europe, and Japan have also added to gloomy predictions for the region, including Venezuela.

Venezuela does not receive any significant foreign investment from the United States or other countries that have been hard-hit by the financial crisis and economic slowdown. The most important, and practically the only, direct impact of these external events on Venezuela is through oil prices. Petroleum exports are currently about 93 percent of Venezuela's exports.

The relevant question for Venezuela is therefore how far oil prices would have to fall before the country would begin to run an unsustainable current account deficit. This is the binding constraint for developing countries. In other words, the United States, Europe, and Japan will—inasmuch as they choose to do so—pursue expansionary monetary and fiscal policies, including deficit government spending, in order to counteract the current recession. Developing countries can and ideally should do the same, but unlike these rich countries, they face a constraint due to the fact that their national currencies are not "hard" currencies. Therefore, they cannot count on being able to borrow nearly as much, relative to GDP [gross domestic product], or for so long a period of time, as countries with hard currencies, to cover their import needs. For this reason, the current account—not the central government budget, which can be covered in local currency—is the most important and binding constraint on developing countries such as Venezuela in the present situation.

We therefore look at current and projected exports and imports under a range of possible oil prices.

"The relevant question for Venezuela is therefore how far oil prices would have to fall before the country would begin to run an unsustainable current account deficit."

Exports

[Data from the Central Bank of Venezuela] show Venezuelan export revenues under various oil price scenarios. For simplicity, we assume that non-oil exports, which are about 7 percent of export revenues, remain constant at $6.5 billion per year.

The Upper Bound: 2.89 Million Barrels per Day

For the volume of exports, we show export levels of 2.62 and 2.89 million barrels per day. The larger number is reported in PDVSA's [Petróleos de Venezuela, S.A., the state-owned petroleum company] most recent financial report. There has been some dispute about how much oil Venezuela exports, with some press reports claiming that the true number is as low as 1.7 million barrels per day. In order to check the accuracy of PDVSA's reporting, we first compared PDVSA's export numbers with import figures for the largest countries that import oil from Venezuela. The U.S. Energy Information Administration reports OECD [Organisation for Economic Co-operation and Development] imports from Venezuela to be 2.0 million barrels per day. In an independent financial statement, PDVSA reports exporting the same amount to OECD countries. China is the other large market for Venezuelan petroleum. While China has not released complete import figures for 2007 or 2008, the Chinese Ministry of Commerce reported in May of 2008 that China was importing 350 thousand barrels per day from Venezuela in 2007, which matches PDVSA's reported exports to China. Thus, there does not appear to be any basis for the claim that Venezuela's oil exports are overstated by PDVSA. We take PDVSA's reported exports, 2.89 million barrels per day, as the upper bound of export volume. . . .

The Lower Bound: 2.62 Million Barrels per Day

With PDVSA's reported export volume confirmed, the only remaining necessary adjustment is to account for PetroCaribe, a program that sells oil on credit, with highly favorable financing terms, to 13 Caribbean nations. Since at least some of this oil does not generate current revenue, and the purpose of the accounting in this [viewpoint] is to estimate Venezuela's current account balance, we can subtract some of this oil from the export totals. No more than half of the oil exported through PetroCaribe is financed through deferred payments, so we can discount half of Venezuela's exports to the Caribbean region, in order to derive a conservative estimate for a lower bound of export volume.

PDVSA's most recent financial statement puts exports to Caribbean countries at 0.54 million barrels per day. Subtracting half of this amount (0.27 million barrels per day) from our upper bound gives a lower bound of 2.62 million barrels per day.

[Data from the International Monetary Fund and the Venezuelan Bank] show Venezuela's export revenue based on these two estimates of oil export volume, for prices ranging from $60 to $90 per barrel for Venezuela's oil. Venezuela's oil sold for 10.4 percent less than the benchmark West Texas Intermediate (WTI) price in 2007. The current price for WTI oil is $65.66; estimates from Goldman Sachs, Merrill Lynch, and the International Energy Agency predict WTI prices of between $80 and $100 per barrel for 2009.

Imports and Trade Balances

... Imports for 2008 are running at an annual rate of $43.2 billion. If the price of Venezuelan oil stays approximately the same for the next two months, then the average price for 2008 will be $90.37, thus providing export revenue of 92.9 to 101.8 billion dollars for 2008, corresponding to exports of 2.62 to 2.89 million barrels per day. This would yield a trade surplus of 49.7 to 58.6 billion dollars for 2008, or an enormous 15.0 to 17.7 percent of GDP, assuming $43.2 billion in imports.

"It is clear that Venezuela can be expected to run current account surpluses for the foreseeable future, even at oil prices far below the levels that are currently forecasted."

For 2009, taking first the high range of projected prices for Venezuela's oil—$90—we get export revenue of between $92.6 to 101.4 billion (again based on 2.62 to 2.89 barrels per day). This results in a trade surplus of between $46.4 and 55.2 billion, or a very large 10.5 to 12.5 percent of GDP. (For these estimates we assume that imports grow by 7 percent annually). For 2010, we get a trade surplus between $43.1 and 51.9 billion, or 7.2 to 8.7 percent of GDP.

As can be seen ..., if the price of Venezuelan oil falls to $80 a barrel, the country would still run a huge trade surplus of 8.4 to 10.1 percent of GDP for 2009, and 5.6 to 6.1 percent of GDP for 2010. At $70 a barrel, this surplus is still large at 6.2 to 7.8 percent of GDP for 2009, and 4.0 to 5.2 percent of GDP for 2010. At $60 a barrel, this surplus is reduced to 3.7 to 5.4 percent of GDP for 2009, and 2.4 to 3.4 percent of GDP for 2010.

Even at $50 per barrel, Venezuela would still run trade surpluses through 2010. However, this is considered to be an extremely unlikely scenario by economists who forecast oil prices.

The current account surplus for 2007 was $20.0 billion, as compared to a trade surplus of $23.7 billion. Thus, including the other items in the current account does not alter the basic picture. Venezuela's foreign debt is only 9 percent of GDP, and interest payments on the debt are 2.2 percent of GDP, or currently $7.4 billion annually. There are no principal payments due on global bonds either this year or next.

It is clear that Venezuela can be expected to run current account surpluses for the foreseeable future, even at oil prices far below the levels that are currently forecasted by any experts in the field. However, even if the economy were to somehow fall into a current account deficit, the government has $40 billion in reserves at the Central Bank and another $37 billion in other hard currency assets. These reserves amount to 23 percent of GDP, thus providing an enormous cushion for any unanticipated events.

"It is therefore important that the [Venezuelan] government consider taking the appropriate fiscal stimulus measures ... to avoid unnecessary declines in the rate of growth of output and employment."

Venezuela Is in a Good Position

In light of the above data, it is difficult to foresee a scenario in which oil prices would fall far enough for Venezuela to run up

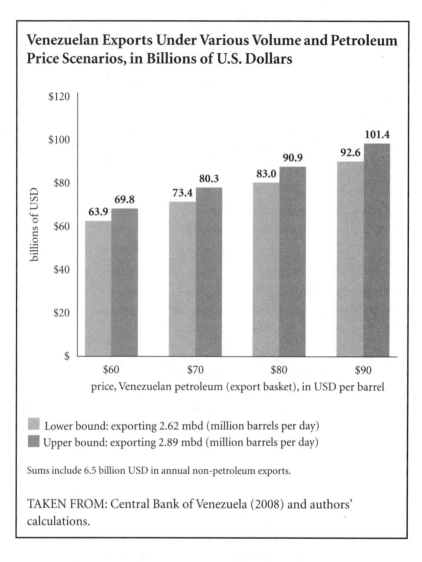

Venezuelan Exports Under Various Volume and Petroleum Price Scenarios, in Billions of U.S. Dollars

Lower bound: exporting 2.62 mbd (million barrels per day)
Upper bound: exporting 2.89 mbd (million barrels per day)

Sums include 6.5 billion USD in annual non-petroleum exports.

TAKEN FROM: Central Bank of Venezuela (2008) and authors' calculations.

against foreign exchange constraints due to loss of export revenue. Clearly, there is also room for imports to grow faster than we assumed here, and Venezuela would still have current account surpluses under foreseeable scenarios. Also, the Venezuelan government controls access to foreign exchange, and could limit the growth of imports if it needed to, although there would not seem to be any need for this in the foreseeable future.

For these reasons, the government should be fully able to pursue an expansionary fiscal policy in order to make up for any slowdown in consumer or capital spending, and keep the economy growing at a healthy pace. Problems with inflation can be expected to subside, since the price of imported goods can be expected to fall as a result of a rapidly decelerating global economy. The price of food commodities has dropped dramatically alongside of oil. Although as noted above there are few direct transmission mechanisms of the global financial crisis and economic slowdown to the Venezuelan economy, the first half of 2008 has shown a fall in capital spending (some of which appears to be government capital spending). Also there will likely be some cutbacks in private spending due to falling confidence in the regional and world economies, generally.

It is therefore important that the government consider taking the appropriate fiscal stimulus measures, including deficit spending as necessary, to avoid unnecessary declines in the rate of growth of output and employment. In the past, developing countries have too often taken pro-cyclical measures—i.e., tighter fiscal and monetary policies—that have worsened economic slowdowns brought on by external shocks. An important exception has been China, which grew rapidly right through the last major financial crisis (1998–2000) while its neighbors suffered huge losses in output and employment. China's success was a result of expansionary fiscal and monetary policy, especially the hundreds of billions of dollars that the government invested in infrastructure during this period. China is now pursuing similar policies in response to the current world slowdown; this week [November 2008] the government announced a $587 billion stimulus package—about 7 percent of GDP—over the next two years.

As noted above, developing countries have often been held back from pursuing the appropriate fiscal and monetary policies in the face of slowing aggregate demand, due to foreign exchange constraints. It is clear from the above data that Venezuela is far from experiencing such constraints and is unlikely to run into them in the foreseeable future.

U.S. Ambassador in Turkmenistan Advocates Security for the International Oil Supply

George Krol

George Krol headed the U.S. delegation at the International Oil and Gas Conference in Turkmenistan. In the following speech, Krol underscores the need for global cooperation to secure the international oil supply. Central Asia is a microcosm of U.S. energy security policy and broader foreign policy. It is U.S. policy to respect the sovereignty and independence of the countries in the region, but also to support increasing and diversifying trade ties in the region in addition to maintaining traditional trade ties. Trade promotes stability and cooperation within the region that can leverage the varying natural resource assets of each country.

As you read, consider the following questions:

1. According to Krol, who benefits from ensuring the reliability and stability of the international energy supply?
2. According to the author, what are the elements of the U.S. domestic and international energy security strategy?
3. According to Krol, what pipelines in Central Asia has the United States helped to create?

George Krol, "Reliable and Stable Transit of Energy and the Role of Energy in Sustainable Development and International Cooperation," Turkmenistan.USembassy.gov, April 24, 2009. U.S. Department of State, Washington, DC.

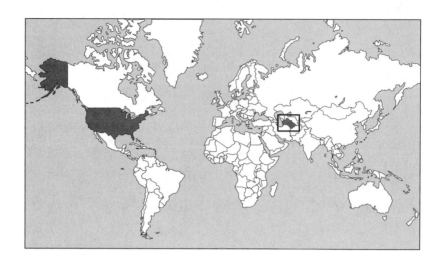

Thank you for this opportunity to say a few words on behalf of the United States of America.

I would like to begin by thanking the government of Turkmenistan for hosting this conference today and for sponsoring last year's UN General Assembly resolution on today's subject—a resolution my government proudly co-sponsored.

Both the resolution and today's conference draw attention to an issue that is of vital and increasing importance to all of us gathered here today.

As a net energy exporter, countries like our host Turkmenistan rely on predictable, diversified, secure, and transparent energy markets to derive the fullest benefits from their natural riches, to anticipate and plan for future infrastructure investment needs, and to maximize access to both established and emerging markets worldwide.

Net importers like my own and many other countries represented here today rely on those same predictable, secure, diversified, and transparent market principles to develop reliable import contracts, anticipate market-driven price and supply fluctuations, and manage a long-term energy security strategy.

In other words, energy security policy is not a competition between producers and consumers. All of us—producers, transit countries, and consumers of energy—benefit from a system that provides transparency and security. The same principles that make energy markets work best for energy exporters are those that provide the foundation for sound energy policy for energy importers. The fact that both producers and consumers are coming together today to discuss these ideas in one room reflects growing acknowledgement of the many benefits we both can derive from this common understanding. Above all, such discussions can lead to more efficient markets that benefit ultimately our peoples and the global economy and global environment—natural, political, and economic.

"Secure access to energy is also central to facilitating economic growth. In a world of increasing demand for energy resources, expanding access to energy and enhancing security of supply are a crucial part of ensuring reliable and stable deliveries of energy resources to international markets."

Energy infrastructure, including transit security, is essential both to producers and consumers. By reducing our vulnerability to the impact of natural and man-made disasters, changes in political situations, threats posed by terrorism, and energy theft, infrastructure security lays the foundation for stability key to well-functioning markets.

Secure access to energy is also central to facilitating economic growth. In a world of increasing demand for energy resources, expanding access to energy and enhancing security of supply are a crucial part of ensuring reliable and stable deliveries of energy resources to international markets.

The energy security concerns this conference is designed to discuss are strongly incorporated in my country's foreign policy. Our international energy security strategy is inextricably linked to our domestic energy security strategy. Both advocate for: (1) greater diversity of energy sources; (2) wise use of energy through efficiency and conservation; (3) a diversity of secure and reliable energy supply routes; and (4) a diversity of energy suppliers working in an open and transparent energy marketplace free from political pressure.

In this time of fragile global financial and economic health, it is more important than ever to have a reliable international energy supply. Greater energy interconnectivity, as well as greater diversity, competitiveness, and transparency in energy markets, will help propel economic recovery and development and increase energy security overall.

The prosperity and security of each of our countries are intrinsically linked to secure, reliable, and diverse supplies of energy. The United States fully supports the efforts represented here today to think strategically and to develop a vision for improving the global energy infrastructure.

A microcosm of our international energy security policy, as well as the interplay between energy security and broader foreign policy, is contained in the very region where we are meeting today—Central Asia. For that reason, I'd like to say a few words about how my government views this region.

"At the same time, we continually highlight the potential for and benefits of regional cooperation in Central Asia, which we believe will foster long-term, durable stability."

A basic tenet of U. S. foreign policy in Central Asia—one which also impacts our energy policy—is to respect the sovereignty and independence of the countries in the region. We want to support partnerships throughout Eurasia, and we will advocate for those partnerships that respect the sovereign states in the region.

We acknowledge the need for interdependence that facilitates trade and investment among countries, but the United

States also believes that a country's sovereignty, independence, and prosperity are best enhanced and protected by increasing and diversifying trade ties. For this reason we strongly support the diversification of energy markets and transit routes, both among Central Asian states and between this region and broader international markets. Diversification does not come at the expense of long standing, traditional trade ties. Rather diversification can enhance these ties and provide efficiencies overall.

At the same time, we continually highlight the potential for and benefits of regional cooperation in Central Asia, which we believe will foster long-term, durable stability. Such inter-action can facilitate expanded trade and economic prosperity, coordination on the use of crucial resources such as water and minerals, and in a number of other areas.

Since energy endowments differ among the countries of the region, there is potential for significant synergies in the energy sector as well. Some states in the region have tremen-dous potential as oil and gas producers, and others are rich in hydroelectric generation possibilities. Improved regional coop-eration can leverage these comparative advantages in a way that benefits everyone, producers and consumers, and that contributes to a stable and prosperous regional economy.

Looking beyond Central Asia to global markets, pipeline and market diversification offers tremendous opportunities for both suppliers and importers. For instance, access to a stable and secure energy supply is one of the biggest chal-lenges faced by firms seeking to operate in South Asia. Energy exports from Central Asia can offset this challenge while bring-ing increased growth and prosperity to the exporting states themselves.

That is one reason my country is an active participant in the effort to create a transmission corridor for electricity from Central to South Asia. Getting Central Asian-generated elec-tricity to South Asia requires progress in Afghanistan, and the

United States has been working actively with the international donor community to increase the availability of electricity in Afghanistan and to develop its resources.

Another area for regional energy cooperation with tremendous potential lies in the Caspian basin.

The U. S. helped in creating the Baku-Tbilisi-Ceyhan oil pipeline and the South Caucasus Pipeline to bring energy exports from the Caspian Basin to markets.

Kazakhstan already ships substantial amounts of oil via Azerbaijan to world markets. We hope to see that energy trade expanded and encourage the growing dialogue between Azerbaijan and our host, Turkmenistan.

Free market forces are key to developing the world's energy resources, and tapping those forces will require tapping into the expertise of international energy firms.

"We continue to believe that diversification, conservation, and investment in technology, and transparent marketplaces that give adequate space for private capital will help the region and the world economy by meeting and managing efficiently the growing demand for energy."

In Central Asia, American and other private companies have the required technical expertise to handle the high sulfur, high temperature, high pressure and depth challenges that are often involved in developing gas fields in this region. Cooperating with the private sector in upstream investment and in expanding transit and export capacity is the most efficient and cost-effective means of capturing the full potential of the region's natural resources.

The United States has long supported energy sector reform and regional energy cooperation in Central Asia. We emphasize sound regulatory frameworks, modernization, investment, and regional energy market development. We continue to believe that diversification, conservation, and invest-

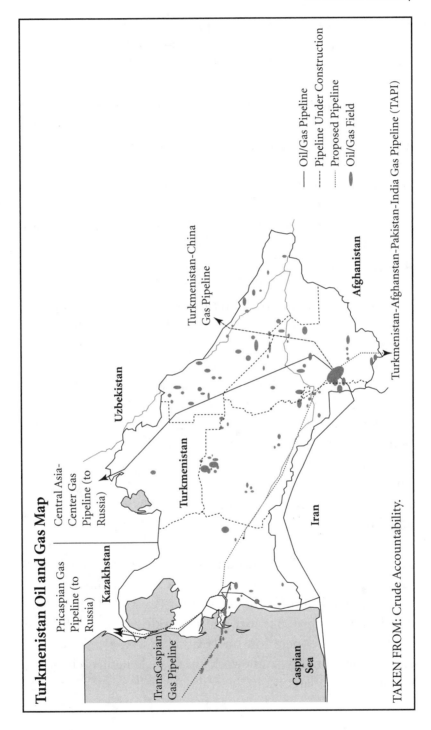

Turkmenistan Oil and Gas Map

Pricaspian Gas Pipeline (to Russia)

Kazakhstan

Central Asia-Center Gas Pipeline (to Russia)

TransCaspian Gas Pipeline

Uzbekistan

Turkmenistan-China Gas Pipeline

Turkmenistan

Afghanistan

Turkmenistan-Afghanistan-Pakistan-India Gas Pipeline (TAPI)

Iran

Caspian Sea

— Oil/Gas Pipeline
--- Pipeline Under Construction
····· Proposed Pipeline
◆ Oil/Gas Field

TAKEN FROM: Crude Accountability.

ment in technology, and transparent marketplaces that give adequate space for private capital will help the region and the world economy by meeting and managing efficiently the growing demand for energy.

Specifically in regard to what American energy policy will look like under the Obama Administration, I would note that a balanced approach to global energy security is at the forefront of the Administration's policy. This is evidenced by the early appointment of Ambassador Richard Morningstar as our Special Envoy for Eurasian Energy.

This appointment of a Special Envoy reflects the high priority the Obama Administration places on cooperation and dialogue on energy issues. Ambassador Morningstar could not be here today but he asked me to send all of you his sincere regrets that he could not attend this important conference due a prior commitment to participate in this week's Sofia Energy Summit. He is, however, no stranger to Ashgabat or Central Asia. I remember traveling with him myself to Ashgabat in the mid 1990s. Ambassador Morningstar anticipates visiting the region shortly and looks forward to meeting many of you.

I will leave the more detailed discussion of our energy policy to Ambassador Morningstar when he meets with you in the future. But I can assure you he is very well aware of the importance and potential of this region and of the importance of energy security. And he is most anxious to work with all of you.

In conclusion, I once again wish to thank the wise and far-seeing leadership of Turkmenistan for hosting this important discussion and drawing attention to the issue of energy security. Thank you for the opportunity to speak to you today. The United States looks forward to working with all of you to continue our cooperation on creating a secure, reliable, and stable global energy framework that can benefit each of our countries and mankind in general.

Saudi Arabia's Oil Capacity Is Disputed

Syed Rashid Husain

Syed Rashid Husain is a contributor to the Arab News. *In the following viewpoint, he outlines the contradictory assessments of Saudi oil capacity, stating that while most Saudi experts believe that the country has significant oil supplies for the near future, many outside observers foresee a decreasing supply. Husain asserts that the data need to be evaluated because action needs to be taken on the matter.*

As you read, consider the following questions:

1. On what did Abdallah Salem El-Badri blame the oil crisis myth?
2. According to Husain, the giant Khurais oil field in Saudi Arabia holds how many billion barrels of oil?
3. How many million barrels of oil a day does the author say the Khurais oil field will produce?

Crude demand-supply balance is definitely tight, no one argues. The spare cushion has perilously gone down to two percent from six percent a few years back. Galloping consumption in the emerging economies of Asia coupled with rising demand within the Arab Gulf has contributed to tight markets.

Syed Rashid Husain, "Of 'Myth' of a Shortage and Saudi Capacity," *Arab News*, July 18, 2008. *Arab News* © 2003 All rights reserved. Reproduced by permission.

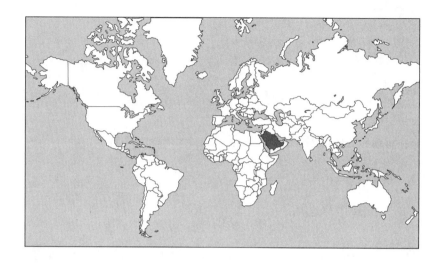

Half-Baked Theories Abound

Skepticism appears ruling the sentiments. Pundits continue churning out various, cooked and semi-cooked, theories about the Saudi capacity to sustain and increase its production from the current levels. Matthew Simmons [a leading expert on peak oil] and his disciples term the Saudi announcement to take production to 12.5 million bpd [barrels per day] by next year, and 15 million bpd if and when required, as "a bunch of empty boasts."

Confusion about the sustainability of some of the major Saudi oil continues to haunt. Debate about the super, giant Saudi fields, so essential for meeting the global energy needs, abound.

And this is confusing the entire world—somewhat unnecessarily—many here in Dhahran, the virtual global energy capital, strongly believe. And it would have serious consequences for the entire world, most agree. Every one including Custodian of the Two Holy Mosques King Abdullah [of Saudi Arabia] also wants and emphasizes on the need of lower oil prices.

OPEC Confronts the Oil Shortage Myth

It was perhaps in this perspective that the secretary general of the Organization of the Petroleum Exporting Countries (OPEC), Abdallah Salem El-Badri, recently denounced the "myth" of an oil shortage and blamed the crisis on speculation sparked by the subprime lending crisis in the United States. "Seventy percent of crude contracts on the NYMEX are held by speculators.... Some form of regulation is needed," he emphasized, adding, "The market has no shortage of physical crude."

"Confusion about the sustainability of some of the major Saudi oil continues to haunt."

On the forefront of the current Saudi drive is the giant Khurais oil field, about 90 miles east of Riyadh. The field holds 27 billion barrels of oil—more than all the proven reserves of the United States. Starting June 2009, it would produce 1.2 million barrels a day, enough to satisfy the projected growth in global demand next year. The Kingdom [of Saudi Arabia] is investing more than $10 billion on the field, with 26 contractors, 106 subcontractors and 28,000 employees working on the mammoth task. It is the largest piece of a five-year, $60-billion effort to expand the Saudi oil production capacity.

New Technology Aids Oil Extraction Efforts

A variety of new technologies, including multiple lateral wells and microscopic robots swimming through rock pores deep underground, will allow Saudi Arabia to start recovering much more of the oil from its fields, says Muhammad Saggaf, the head of [Saudi] Aramco's advanced exploration research wing. Consequently, it is expected that the amount of recoverable crude, from the fields could go up to 70 percent from the current 50 percent over the next 20 years; Saggaf was quoted as saying, adding another 80 billion barrels to the Saudi reserves.

Saudi Arabia insists it would be able to pump at 12.5 million barrels per day for as long as the market needs once new capacity comes online next year, a Saudi oil official was quoted as saying earlier this week [July 2008].

"This is sustainable for as long as the market needs it," he said. "We are on track to reach production capacity of 12.5 million bpd by the middle of next year and we will do it." The Kingdom is pumping at the highest rate since 1981, and has boosted output by 550,000 bpd since May. OPEC pumped an average 32.47 million barrels per day of crude oil in June, up 230,000 bpd from May, industry tracker Platts reported Tuesday in its latest survey.

In June, OPEC exports were reported at considerably higher levels. Higher volumes from Saudi Arabia accounted for almost all of the increase, Platts reported. Saudi Arabia produced an average 9.45 million bpd, up 210,000 bpd from the previous month.

The 12 OPEC members bound by output agreements, which exclude Iraq, pumped an average 29.98 million bpd in June, up from 29.75 million bpd in May, and above their 29.673 million bpd output target.

Naysayers Counter OPEC Claims

However, not everyone seems convinced by the Saudi and the OPEC gestures and some continue to stay skeptic. What could then be done? The issue of sustainable supplies and future capacity continue to cloud the horizon with some warning new tensions from 2010. In order to dissipate these clouds, the International Energy Agency (IEA) has undertaken a mammoth project of auditing the super giant wells of the world so as to evaluate the supply side of the balance.

State of Saudi Oil Reserves

Saudi Arabia has over 300 recognized reservoirs, but 90% of its oil comes from the five super giant fields discovered between 1940 and 1965. Since the 1970s there haven't been new discoveries of giant fields. The most significant of the oil fields is Ghawar. Found in 1948, the 300-mile-long sliver near the Persian Gulf is the world's largest oil field and accounts for 55–60% of all Saudi oil produced. Ghawar's current proven reserves are 12% of the world's total. The field produces 5 mbd [million barrels per day], which is 6.25% of the world's oil production.

Institute for the Analysis of Global Security,
"New Study Raises Doubts About Saudi Oil Reserves,"
Energy Security, *March 31, 2004.*

The field by field report of the IEA is scheduled to be released in November this year and reportedly Fatih Birol [chief economist at the IEA] and his team seem to be burning the proverbial midnight lamp, in order to compile their report in time. Fatih though prefers to remain tight-lipped on the issue, until the final report is out.

"The issue of sustainable supplies and future capacity continue to cloud the horizon."

But now another report has hit the energy fraternity. The influential *BusinessWeek*, on the basis of some 'fresh data on Saudi Arabia's oil fields,' now claims that for at least the next five years, and possibly longer, the Kingdom is likely to produce less than the promised 12.5 million barrels a day.

The detailed document, reportedly obtained by *Business-Week* from a person with access to Saudi oil officials, suggests that Saudi Aramco will be limited to sustained production of just 12 million barrels a day in 2010, and will be able to maintain that volume only for short, temporary periods such as emergencies. Then it will scale back to a sustainable production level of about 10.4 million barrels a day.

Report Details

BusinessWeek claims it has obtained a field-by-field breakdown of estimated Saudi oil production from 2009 through 2013. It was provided by an oil industry executive who said he had confirmed it with a ranking Saudi energy official who has access to the field data.

The data about Ghawar, the super giant Saudi field, shows it producing 5.4 million barrels a day next year, "but the volume then falling off rapidly, to 4.475 million daily barrels in 2013. That's why Khurais is so important to make up for that decrease," said the oil industry executive who generated the data.

Indeed how fresh are the data and how authentic the source remains to be evaluated. The two sides but are poles apart—ominous by any means—and something needs to be done rather urgently.

Periodical Bibliography

The following articles have been selected to supplement the diverse views presented in this chapter.

Roy Clancy — "No Sermons Needed on Oilsands," *Ottawa Sun*, May 20, 2009.

Cliff Coonan — "China's Thirst for Oil Has Multiple Agendas," *National*, November 3, 2009.

Rhonda Duey — "Learning from Past Mistakes," *E&P*, January 5, 2009.

Rhonda Duey — "Operators to U.K.—Lower the Cost of Doing Business!" *E&P*, September 11, 2009.

Nick Mathiason — "Developed Countries Face Threat of Soaring Prices and Food Shortages," *Observer*, November 1, 2009.

Wang Qian — "Oil and Coal Imports Signal Recovery," *China Daily*, October 22, 2009.

Kevin Rafferty — "Reactive Oil Markets Won't Wait," *Japan Times*, June 27, 2009.

Louise Redvers — "Oil-Rich Angola Looks to Diversify Economy to Avoid Slump," *Mail & Guardian Online*, February 17, 2009.

Michael Richardson — "Who Can Win on Oil Slicks?" *Japan Times*, January 9, 2009.

Martin Saatdjian — "Capitalist vs. Socialist State Intervention of the Economy," Venezuelanalysis.com, October 1, 2008.

Ashley Seager — "A Post-Oil World Gets Less Sci-Fi by the Day," *Guardian*, October 26, 2009.

David Wighton — "Long-Term Power of Oil Is Open to Doubt," *Times Online*, October 6, 2009.

Oil and the Environment

China Faces Challenges on Economic Development and Environmental Protections

Noeleen Heyzer

Noeleen Heyzer is executive secretary of the United Nations Economic and Social Commission for Asia and the Pacific (ESCAP). In the following viewpoint, she elucidates the significant economic strides the Asia-Pacific region has made in the past few decades. She asserts that in order to remain a global player in the world economy, countries like China must be innovative and forward-thinking when it comes to environmental issues, particularly carbon emissions and climate change.

As you read, consider the following questions:

1. According to the author, what percentage of Asia-Pacific's energy needs are fulfilled by fossil fuels?
2. How many people do not have access to electricity in the Asia-Pacific region, according to Heyzer?
3. For what percentage of the global greenhouse gas emissions does the author say the Asia-Pacific region is accountable?

Asia-Pacific's economic and social progress over the past few decades has achieved remarkable results, including lifting millions of people out of poverty. And despite the glo-

Noeleen Heyzer, "Riding High on a Low-Carbon Economy," *China Daily*, June 30, 2009. Reproduced by permission.

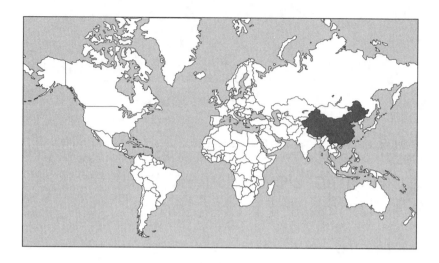

bal economic crisis there is every reason to believe the Asia-Pacific region will remain dynamic and continue to contribute to global economic recovery and growth, and help alleviate poverty. While world leaders race to tackle the economic crisis, it is important to review the lessons we have learned in order to find how long-term recovery can be achieved.

Oil Price Volatility Causes Problems

Volatile oil prices last year [2008] were a sobering reminder of Asia's high dependency on energy, particularly fossil fuels, for development. In fact 80 percent of Asia-Pacific's energy comes from fossil fuels. The peaking of oil prices at $147 a barrel last year, and soaring of food and commodity prices sent alarm bells ringing across many developing countries in the region.

In fact, energy poses a number of challenges in Asia-Pacific, which is characterized by significant disparities in energy consumption. About 1.7 billion people in the region still rely on traditional biomass for cooking and heating, and 1 billion do not have access to electricity. As a result, children cannot study at night and adults cannot power their small businesses or run much-needed medical services in these areas.

Since energy drives development, the neglected sections of our population need reliable sources of energy if they are to help the economy prosper.

Oil Consumption and Environmental Concerns

We know energy is needed to maintain economic growth, reduce poverty and achieve the UN [United Nations] Millennium Development Goals. But we also know climate change is intrinsically linked to energy production and consumption, and the more fossil fuels we use, the more damage we cause to our planet.

Asia-Pacific accounts for 34 percent of the global greenhouse gas (GHG) emissions, with most of it coming from the consumption of fossil fuels. The region's share of energy-related GHG emissions is expected to increase to 47 percent by 2030 if the present development trend continues. The resulting impact on agriculture, rising sea levels and growing severe weather patterns could hurt the region's economic development severely.

"Climate change . . . offers a historic opportunity to restructure our approach to development and make it more economically, socially and ecologically balanced."

Thus, Asia-Pacific, and indeed the rest of the world, faces a dilemma. How do we ensure all people, including the poor, have access to safe, reliable supplies of energy without undermining environmental resources essential for our survival?

Climate change is not only the most daunting challenge of our times, but also offers a historic opportunity to restructure our approach to development and make it more economically, socially and ecologically balanced.

Opportunities Arise in Energy Innovation

The UN Economic and Social Commission for Asia and the Pacific [ESCAP], the regional arm of the UN, has been promoting low-carbon, green growth investments in new and renewable sources of energy, energy-efficiency projects and clean technologies. Though people's understanding of a low-carbon approach is still evolving, there are a number of areas where the concept can be clearly applied.

The Asia-Pacific region is home to a number of important energy exporters and importers, but it does not have an integrated energy market. This necessitates the setting up of a trans-Asian energy network to facilitate cross-border flow of energy, technologies and services, and leverage existing fossil fuel and electricity markets to tap into unrealized efficiency areas.

Such a network will require trust and cooperation among neighboring countries, which have to come up with favorable policies, technical help and interconnected infrastructure.

Environmentally sound technologies are essential to the fight against climate change and environmental degradation. Countries like Japan, the Republic of Korea (ROK), India and China have become big global players. Their governments have been supporting clean technologies by enforcing effective policies and regulatory arrangements, and promoting investments and R&D [research and development] both in public and private sectors.

Forging public-private partnerships will play a key role in the commercialization of these new technologies, while intra-regional trade will increase the level of their adoption.

Fundamental Changes Are Needed

The way energy is used has to be changed fundamentally if we want to shift toward low-carbon development. The region's energy demand is expected to reach 9 trillion dollars according to current prices by 2030, which energy-related industries, including those generating renewable energy, could cash in on. For example, the development of smart electrical grids will make energy use more efficient and create an environment for growth of renewable energy.

City planning, infrastructure building and service provision, too, have to undergo fundamental change. Cities should have high-density areas that promote public transport, and bicycle and green corridors. New buildings have to be energy-efficient, and should have better provisions of water and energy, and an efficient system to collect and recycle wastes. Last but not least, cities should offer economy housing to the poor.

"The way energy is used has to be changed fundamentally."

Making energy accessible to all will help alleviate poverty and promote inclusive and sustainable development. This will require putting in place social safety nets to cope with disruptions in energy supply. It will also require partnerships among governments, businesses and NGOs [nongovernmental organizations] to raise resources and ensure equitable distribution of energy among the poor and low-income families.

The Asia-Pacific Region Is in the Forefront

A number of countries in the Asia-Pacific region such as China, the ROK, Japan and Australia have adopted the concept of low-carbon development. And negotiators are racing against time to reach a new global deal on climate change in Copenhagen in December [2009].

It's in such a backdrop that the June 17–20 [2009] Asia-Pacific Forum on Low Carbon Economy brought together government officials, technical experts and businesses in Beijing to discuss how to achieve low-carbon development in China and the rest of the Asia-Pacific region. Organized by ESCAP in partnership with the National Development and

Reform Commission of China and WWF [World Wildlife Fund], the forum created a platform for decision makers to share their experiences and develop new strategies.

The region needs to develop a vision that is inclusive and sustainable to join the rest of the world in tackling the economic crisis. Huge stimulus packages and policy reforms being put together by governments in the region provide an unprecedented opportunity to turn these ideas into action.

Japan Is Weaning Itself from Big Oil and Plans to Lower Carbon Emissions

Stephen Hesse

Stephen Hesse is a professor at Chuo Law School in Tokyo, Japan, and an environmental columnist for the Japan Times. *In the following viewpoint, he observes that while Americans argue whether climate change exists at all, the Japanese government has commissioned a team of researchers to work on cutting-edge scenarios for a low-carbon society. Hesse applauds Japan's bold and visionary role in confronting climate change.*

As you read, consider the following questions:

1. According to Hesse, what U.S. states have passed landmark legislation requiring 80 percent cuts in emissions of greenhouse gases by 2050?
2. As stated in the viewpoint, in what year did the Japan Low Carbon Society Scenarios project begin?
3. According to the sustainability report, to what extent will we need to cut greenhouse gas emissions by 2050 in order to stabilize the global climate within natural fluctuations?

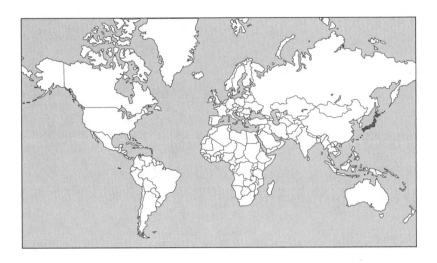

How can an economic superpower founded on progress and innovation be so averse to change that would cut the greenhouse gas emissions that are spurring global warming and climate change?

While the Japanese government now has a team of researchers working on scenarios for a low-carbon society, politicians and corporations in the United States remain polarized over whether warming is worth worrying about.

My guess is that future generations will be dumbfounded at how long it took us, in the face of such certainty, to get over our self-destructive fixation on generating energy from fossil fuels.

"Future generations will be dumbfounded at how long it took us . . . to get over our self-destructive fixation on generating energy from fossil fuels."

More than a Glimmer of Hope

Still, there's hope. A recent report released in Japan illustrates that major cuts in CO_2 emissions can be made without compromising economic growth, by reducing energy demand and moving to a low-carbon energy supply.

Apparently, several U.S. states recognize this as well. California, Minnesota and New Jersey have all passed landmark legislation requiring 80 percent cuts in greenhouse gas emissions by 2050. At the national level of U.S. politics, however, oil- and car-company lobbyists still have more clout than voters.

Luckily, the rest of the world is not nearly so wedded to the past, nor so beholden to Big Oil.

Some Countries Are Taking Action

Japan and Europe, for example, have moved beyond bickering between the two camps—those who profit from inaction, and those developing new energy approaches that make environmental and economic sense. In Japan, government-backed researchers have begun "back-casting" from 2050 in an effort to calculate what steps should be taken over the next 40 years to achieve a 70 percent cut in CO_2 emissions by then.

This back-casting is part of a research project known as the Japan Low Carbon Society [LCS] Scenarios Toward 2050. The project began in 2004 under the auspices of the National Institute of Environmental Studies and Kyoto University, and is funded by the Global Environmental Research Fund of the Ministry of the Environment. It includes about 60 researchers and experts from universities, research institutes and businesses specializing in such fields as environment, energy, economics, industry, transportation and urban studies, writes Kiyoshi Koshiba in the *Japan for Sustainability Newsletter*, issue 59, released July 31 [2007] online.

Koshiba's article summarizes an interim report the research team released this year [2007], titled *Japan Scenarios Towards a Low-Carbon Society (LCS): Feasibility Study for 70 Percent CO_2 Emission Reduction by 2050 below 1990 Level.*

Japan for Sustainability is a nonprofit organization that disseminates environmental information from and about Japan in an effort to promote a more sustainable society. . . .

Report Findings Reveal Challenges

According to the team's report, scientific data confirm that stabilizing the global climate within natural fluctuations will require 50 percent cuts in human greenhouse gas emissions by 2050. Because industrialized countries have the largest emissions per capita—and thus the greatest ethical responsibility to cut greenhouse gases—the researchers have studied the feasibility of creating a dramatically low-carbon society in Japan.

Their conclusion? If Japan reduces its energy demands by 40 to 45 percent through improved efficiency and the introduction of a low-carbon energy supply, the nation has the technological potential to reduce CO_2 emissions to 70 percent below 1990 levels by 2050, without sacrificing its present levels of affluence.

Beginning with a vision of a desirable Japanese society in 2050, the researchers established two scenarios with differing goals: Scenario A focuses on technologies and economic growth, while Scenario B focuses on local communities and the natural environment.

Report Assumptions

Through brainstorming, the researchers detailed the future society, including goods and services needed, architecture and city planning, and changes in industrial structure. They then quantified energy needs. They also made the following assumptions, some of which you will agree with, others you might not:

- First, annual per capita GDP [gross domestic product] would be 2 percent in Scenario A and 1 percent in Scenario B;

- Second, due to Japan's declining birthrate, a baseline population of 127 million (the year 2000) could be expected to decrease to 95 million by 2050 in Scenario A, and to 100 million in Scenario B. Furthermore, in Scenario A, Japan's GDP in 2050 would be double the 2000 level, while in Scenario B it would be about 1.5 times the 2000 level.

Koshiba notes four more assumptions. The level of services necessary for daily life (e.g., clothing, food, housing and entertainment) should be maintained or improved; innovative technologies, such as those for electric or fuel-cell vehicles, should be considered; unproved technologies, such as nuclear fusion, are excluded; and the analysis should be in line with existing long-term national strategies, including plans for nuclear power.

Recognizing the chronic inability of Japan's electrical utilities to use nuclear power safely, paired with government determination to increase nuclear-power generation, this fourth assumption may be a deal-killer for those totally averse to nuclear power.

However, based on these assumptions, here are some of the researchers' conclusions regarding estimated energy-demand reductions:

- The industrial sector should reduce energy demand 20 to 40 percent through structural changes and energy-saving technologies;

- The passenger-transportation sector will need cuts of 80 percent through more efficient land use and improved energy efficiency;

- The freight-transportation sector should reduce by 60 to 70 percent through better logistics management and improved-efficiency vehicles;

- The household sector needs 50 percent cuts in energy use through replacing old buildings, increased use of insulation, and new energy-saving appliances;

- The commercial sector should reduce energy use by 40 percent through renovation and construction, using high-insulation building materials and energy-saving office equipment.

All these reductions sound expensive to implement, but the researchers suggest that Scenario A can be achieved at an annual cost of 1 percent of GDP (based on projections for the year 2050), or between ¥8.9 trillion (0.83 percent of GDP in 2050) and ¥9.8 trillion (0.9 percent); and that Scenario B can be realized at an annual cost of between ¥6.7 trillion (0.96 percent) and ¥7.4 trillion (1.06 percent). A lot, yes—but far less than most countries dole out annually on their military spending.

Early Investment Is Key

Perhaps the researchers' most pertinent finding is the need to make changes sooner rather than later.

"Early investment in energy savings is the optimal path for mitigation action. When energy-saving investments are de-layed . . . it becomes necessary to introduce technologies at a higher marginal cost, and it is estimated that economic loss will be greater than the loss in the case of early investment," notes Koshiba.

"Perhaps the researchers' most pertinent finding is the need to make changes sooner rather than later."

As the researchers conclude, "In order to achieve the LCS goals, . . . prompt action should be taken at the earliest stage. Such action involves structural changes in the industrial sector and investment in infrastructure. Moreover, it is necessary to accelerate development, investment and use of energy-saving technologies and low-carbon energy technologies."

British-Japanese Cooperation Yields Results

Interestingly, Japan is not working alone. According to Koshiba, since February 2006 the Ministry of the Environment in Japan and the Department for Environment, Food and Rural Affairs in Britain have been cooperating on scientific research under the heading, "Developing Visions for a Low-Carbon Society Through Sustainable Development."

In addition to joint research, the Anglo-Japanese project is hosting international workshops to integrate related studies worldwide. Two of these have already been held, and the third will be held in February 2008 in Tokyo. At that meeting, low-carbon studies from around the globe will be consolidated for the 34th G8 [group of eight industrialized countries] summit, scheduled to be held in Japan next July.

"So listen up, America: The future's here, and it's all about more for less carbon."

But if there is one line from Koshiba's summary of the report that U.S. politicians should take to heart, it is this: "The government should play a leading role in promoting a common vision towards LCS at the earliest stage, enforcing comprehensive measures for societal and technological innovation, implementing strong measures for translating such reduction potential into reality, promoting measures for public investment based on long-term perspectives and leading incentives for private investment."

So listen up, America: The future's here, and it's all about more for less carbon.

Canada's Oil Industry Is Committed to Protecting the Environment and Remaining a Global Economic Force

Dave Collyer

Dave Collyer is the president of the Canadian Association of Petroleum Producers (CAPP). (In regard to other short forms in the essay, the terms StatCan and Chamber refer to Statistics Canada and Calgary Chamber of Commerce respectively.) In the following viewpoint, he reviews the considerable commitment the Canadian oil and natural gas industry has made to protect the natural environment and fight global climate change. Collyer also underscores the industry's need to adjust to the changing nature of future North American energy demands and ruminates on the role the industry can play in reviving the North American economy.

As you read, consider the following questions:

1. How much money does Collyer say that the Canadian oil and natural gas industry spent on environmental protection in 2006?

2. According to Collyer, how many jobs are directly and indirectly related to the Canadian oil and natural gas industry?

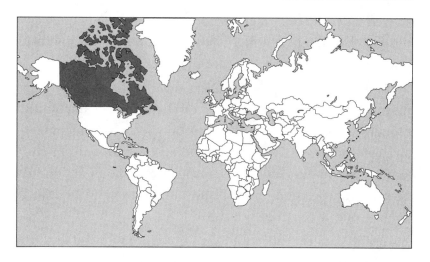

3. A March 2009 Ipsos Reid survey found that what percentage of Canadians feel that the Canadian government should focus on jobs rather than climate change at the moment?

Good morning and thank you for joining us.

Because many of you are colleagues and partners in our industry I know that I will run the risk this morning of being accused of preaching to the choir, but bear with me. I am proud of what our industry has accomplished, I am confident about our future, and I believe that we have common objectives that can help our industry be a leader in the North American economic recovery.

Before going on, I would like to take a moment to express on behalf of CAPP and all of its members our profound sympathy to the families, friends and colleagues of the men and women who lost their lives in the helicopter accident last week off Newfoundland and Labrador. I've been offshore on the East Coast and I know that this is something that the industry thinks about and prepares for, but certainly hopes never happens. These are difficult times for our industry, but all of us are reminded by this tragic incident that nothing is more important than the health and safety of our employees and contractors and those who live near our operations.

You won't be surprised to hear that I will focus my comments today on three areas: environment, energy and economy. I will emphasize the link between economic growth and environmental achievement, because we cannot be reluctant to talk about what has already been accomplished, and how we can position Canada and our industry to be leaders coming out of this recession.

I will take the liberty of doing some myth-busting this morning, because our industry spent $2.8 billion in 2006 on environmental protection—nearly one-third of the $8.6 billion spent by all business in Canada that year, and more than any other industry. We have seen results, and the commitment to environmental performance—real, measurable change in standards and practices—has earned us the right to talk about our role in maintaining and advancing Canada's economic and social well-being. Demonstrated environmental performance also opens the door to an unapologetic discussion about competitiveness.

I hope to leave you this morning with a sense of both opportunity and urgency. But I will resist framing this discussion only in terms of billions of dollars of investment and millions of barrels of oil, because when we talk about meeting the energy needs of Canada and North America we are really talking about people and jobs. . . . At its peak prior to the recession some 500,000 jobs directly and indirectly related to our industry across the country—not just in Alberta or Western Canada. The Canadian Energy Research Institute is about to release a study that will further confirm the very significant role the oil and gas sector will continue to play in economic recovery and future job creation across Canada.

It is critically important that we take a balanced view of our industry in a "3E" context—energy, environment and economy. That will be the focus of my remarks in the next few minutes.

"With a decreasing supply of conventional hydrocarbons, unconventional (both oil and gas) are going to play an increasing role in the energy supply mix."

Context Setting

First, it is important to ground this discussion in an understanding of the role that hydrocarbons will play in the energy mix going forward.

It is popular these days to talk about radically transforming the energy supply mix in a very short period of time and creating abundant employment in the process. It is true that alternative energy sources, including wind, solar, biomass and others, will play an increasingly important role in the energy supply mix. New technologies and increased investment will accelerate this process and will certainly create new jobs.

However, it is also true that global energy demand is projected to increase significantly—forecasts suggest a 50 per cent increase by 2030 and a doubling by 2050—driven by population growth and aspirations for higher standards of living in the developing world. Most reputable forecasters agree that hydrocarbons are going to continue to provide the majority of energy supply over this period. With a decreasing supply of conventional hydrocarbons, unconventional (both oil and gas) are going to play an increasing role in the energy supply mix. In this regard, Western Canada is uniquely positioned to be a key part of the supply equation for some time to come.

To quote from the International Energy Agency's November 2008 report: "These trends call for energy-supply investment of $26.3 trillion to 2030, or over $1 trillion a year." Even as renewables alter the energy mix, the greater part of the world's energy needs—and that $1 trillion a year in investment—will be in hydrocarbons.

I think this reinforces the necessity of a balanced approach to achieving Canada's potential—environmental performance, economic growth and assured energy supply.

"Canadians believe that environmental and economic issues are not mutually exclusive."

Most Canadians understand this. Earlier this month an Ipsos Reid survey found that 71 per cent of Canadians agree that "it is more important for the Canadian government to focus on jobs than climate change at the moment." At the same time, 57 per cent of Canadians agreed that "Canada should take serious action on climate change right now, even if it means higher deficits." And 64 per cent said oil sands development should stop until a clean method of extraction can be found.

That position might come as a surprise to the hundreds of thousands of Canadians who depend on our industry, but there is no question that Canadians believe that environmental and economic issues are not mutually exclusive. Canadians are telling us they think the right balance is achievable and arguably, they are insisting on it. But in any case, we agree: resource development is a fundamental part of our nation's economic future and we must find cleaner methods of extraction and make real progress on greenhouse gas emissions. This is not a case of "either/or." We will need all forms of energy developed responsibly. It can be done, and it is being done.

Environment

When I talk about environmental performance, I often talk about the need to put it in context—relative to the energy security and economic benefits arising from our activity, in terms of relative impact, and in terms of the action that is being taken on mitigation and reclamation. The recent *National Geographic* photo-essay on the oil sands is a case in point. I acknowledged in CAPP's response to the article that "images of oil sands development are inevitably striking. But looking at the larger picture—and understanding the role that new technologies are playing in shaping the future of the oil sands—creates a broader understanding of why this resource is important to Canadians and what the industry is doing to develop it responsibly. What was missing in *National Geographic's* photographs of the boreal forest before and during development is the 'after' picture. What readers do not see is that all oil sands developments are ultimately reclaimed and returned to a natural state." Our objective is not to criticize other jurisdictions—or even a cultural icon like *National Geographic*—but rather to make the case to move forward on a more balanced agenda. I could discuss technological advances and measurable improvement on water use, air quality or land reclamation in some detail, but today I'm going to focus on climate change. I was in Washington late last month shortly after President Obama's visit to Canada, and it is clear that climate change policy is very near the top of the agenda in both the new administration and in Congress. It is also clear that there is considerable uncertainty about the direction the U.S. legislative process will take on this issue and the timing with which policy will move forward.

Having said that, you don't need to spend much time in Washington or in key U.S. states to understand that it is in our best interest to ensure that our southern neighbours recognize as quickly as possible that greenhouse gas emissions are also a high priority for Canada and for our industry.

We cannot afford to be defensive. Canada exported more than 2.4 million barrels a day of oil and refined petroleum products to the United States in 2007. Importantly, and sometimes forgotten in the focus on oil sands, we also provide about 16 per cent of America's natural gas consumption, with potential for significant growth and to play a key role in transitioning the U.S. energy supply portfolio.

"It is in our best interest to ensure that our southern neighbours recognize as quickly as possible that greenhouse gas emissions are also a high priority for Canada and our industry."

Again, context is important. There has been a 33 per cent reduction in greenhouse gas emission intensity in Canada's oil sands since 1990, according to Environment Canada—that's up from an earlier estimate of 27 per cent. Technology improvement accounts for about half of this overall improvement. The oil sands represent just 5 per cent of Canada's total GHG emissions and less than one-tenth of 1 per cent of global emissions. Put another way, greenhouse gas emissions from Canadian oil sands production represent just 0.5 per cent of the total annual GHG emissions of the United States. Closer to home our industry has been subject to Alberta's greenhouse gas legislation since 2007, which requires further reductions in greenhouse gas emissions intensity or a payment of $15/tonne of CO_2. Today, the greenhouse gas intensity of oil sands production in Alberta compares favourably to imports to the United States from other parts of the world including Mexico, Venezuela and even to some U.S. domestic production in California. Despite all of this, the oil sands have become a visible and convenient target—let's be honest, it has become the whipping-boy for the "off oil" movement and GHG concerns. As I stated earlier, we are going to be using significant quantities of hydrocarbons for some time to come, so this perception must be challenged on the facts, it must be put in context and we must remain focused on what is being done now and what will be done in the future to address GHG emissions.

Let me just provide a couple of examples in that regard:

- Syncrude Canada Ltd. and Shell Canada Limited are lowering GHG emissions by advancing technology that reduces the temperature of the process water used to separate the heavy oil from the sand during extraction.

- Other firms are looking at technologies that heat the oil sands using electrical current instead of steam, reducing GHG emissions from production.

- Several companies are testing the ability to partially or completely eliminate the need for steam by injecting solvents, such as propane, into the oil sands to dilute bitumen and allow it to flow.

These are just a few examples of the advancements in technology that are driving, today and in the future, improvements in greenhouse gas emissions from oil sands production. In addition, carbon capture and storage holds promise for addressing emissions that arise from oil sands production. I am very encouraged by the increasing focus on technology development evident in recent announcements from both the U.S. and Canadian governments. The U.S.-Canada Clean Energy Dialogue will create new opportunities for broader engagement in technology development. It is important that our industry be actively engaged and there is clearly an opportunity for cross-border collaboration.

I appreciate that most of you are aware that this work is underway. My point is that we cannot assume that Canadians—and policy makers both north and south of the border—are aware of these advances.

Let me turn now to climate change policy, which is the subject of renewed focus both in Canada and in the United States. There are some key principles that we think are important in the design of any climate change policy:

- It must take a balanced "3E" approach;

- It must provide policy predictability and stability to support longer term investment decisions;

- It must promote the technology development necessary for significant future reductions in greenhouse gas emissions;

- It must align with the policies of our major competitors, or adjust for differences so as not to undermine competitiveness, particularly for energy intensive, trade-exposed sectors; and

- It must allow for regional differences and harmonize across jurisdictions.

"Carbon pricing . . . should be a central element of policy to reduce greenhouse gas emissions efficiently."

Broad carbon pricing designed in accordance with these principles should be a central element of policy to reduce greenhouse gas emissions efficiently. There are many policy designs that can achieve these objectives and we should be much more focused on the substance of the policy rather than the label, whether the latter is "Cap & Trade", "Carbon Tax" or some other variation. What really matters at the end of the day is the price of carbon and how the policy impacts particular sectors or jurisdictions. Our oil and gas sector and Alberta must be actively engaged in climate change policy development, building on what has already been done in this province and ensuring that our interests are represented in the evolving Canadian, bilateral Canada/U.S. and/or international policy frameworks.

We support the view that our enviable and mutually beneficial energy relationship with the United States can provide the foundation for policy development that puts climate

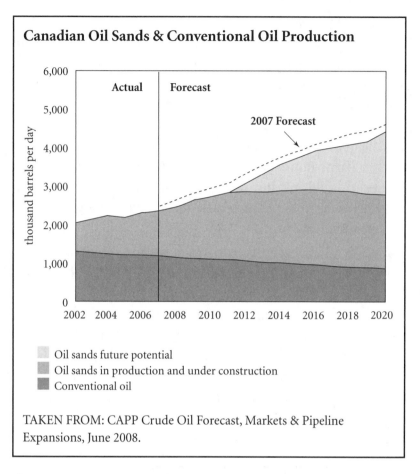

Canadian Oil Sands & Conventional Oil Production

Oil sands future potential
Oil sands in production and under construction
Conventional oil

TAKEN FROM: CAPP Crude Oil Forecast, Markets & Pipeline Expansions, June 2008.

change, economic growth and energy security front and centre on the agenda. We should work toward nothing less.

I won't say anything further about climate change policy, other than to note that the price of carbon is also a competitiveness issue.

Competitiveness

So let's turn now to the subject of competitiveness.

There is no question that activity and jobs have shifted out of Alberta to other onshore jurisdictions in North America over the past year. Recent actions by the Alberta government, including the drilling incentive program announced earlier this month, have been positive steps forward. They consider the tough economic circumstances we currently face and the need to increase oil and gas activity—and that means jobs. However, we have also been frank in saying that, while they are welcome, these short-term measures do not deal with the fundamental issues regarding competitiveness, including royalties that will drive oil and gas activity in the province for the longer term. More broadly, Alberta's future depends on its ability to build investor confidence in the province's resource development sector and to successfully compete globally for scarce capital resources.

We firmly believe that Alberta needs to take a comprehensive and integrated look at the competitiveness of the oil and gas sector relative to other jurisdictions with which it is competing to attract investment. This should certainly address the regulatory framework in the province. An example of this is the appropriateness of the regulatory review process for in situ oil sands projects, where even relatively minor changes in an application can take several months for review. I want to be very clear that this is about the efficiency of the process, not about lowering regulatory review standards.

"All Canadians benefit from oil and gas development."

The review of competitiveness must also address fiscal terms (including income tax, property tax and royalties). This review should be done with a sense of urgency, but needs to be done right. Albertans and the oil and gas industry have a shared stake in the creation of a regulatory process that improves efficiency without lowering standards, and a fiscal framework that will both attract investment back to Alberta and create jobs. I am optimistic that the provincial government recognizes this, and we look forward to working with them to that end.

The stakes are high, underscoring the importance of a leadership role for Canada's oil and gas industry in the economic recovery. Within Canada, $50 billion was invested by our sector in 2007 and 2008—the nation's largest single private sector investor. Investment in 2009 will be somewhat lower—we estimate something in the order of $30 billion to $35 billion—but remains very significant in a national context.

In 2007 our industry contributed an estimated $27 billion to government revenues in the form of royalty payments, land payments and income taxes, ensuring that all Canadians benefit from oil and gas development—dollars supporting health care, education, social services and other programs critical to our standard of living and quality of life.

Yet I think it is fair to say that we have too often taken for granted that Canadians understand the importance of their natural resources. I do not expect *National Geographic* to concern itself with economic growth and job creation, but our industry does not have that option.

Communications

This is a communications challenge—it is *our* challenge—and all of us here today have a stake in rising to that challenge.

Our industry can't allow itself to be drawn into an adversarial debate with detractors who want to shift the focus entirely to the environmental dimension. It is definitely our responsibility to address the mistruths that are out there—and we will do so in a visible and timely manner. However, we will primarily focus on our message, confident that our environmental commitments are not diminished or undermined by recognizing that we must also concern ourselves with economic growth and energy security.

I need to be blunt with regard to the message on jobs and the economy. Statistics Canada reported last week that the unemployment rate has reached 7.7 per cent. In the natural resource sector—mining and oil and gas extraction—some 8,300 jobs were lost in February alone. We have seen this impact in rural Alberta, and it is becoming more evident in Edmonton and Calgary. According to StatCan, Canada has lost 295,000 jobs overall since last October. These are sobering numbers and we should not hesitate to argue that we can be leaders in the economic recovery.

I do not expect to persuade those on the extremes of the energy and environment discussion to seriously consider our perspective, but I do think that we owe it to our industry—and those who benefit from what we do—to be more vocal in challenging narrow positions and misrepresentations that willfully ignore the greater benefits that a balanced approach to the broader range of issues will yield. As I mentioned earlier in the discussion of recent polling data, we believe that the majority of Canadians do in fact subscribe to a more balanced point of view.

Before I close, I want to thank the Chamber and its members for the opportunity to speak today. I'd also like to thank both the CAPP members here today and our industry partners and yes, those who will help keep our feet to the fire.

If there is one thing that most of us have in common, it is a sense of urgency and a desire to emerge from this recession stronger and better positioned for the future. I firmly believe that we can shape a balanced future—one that strikes the right balance between environmental performance, assured energy supply and economic growth. It is our responsibility to commit, to communicate and to act. It can be done, it is being done, and I am confident that it will continue to be done in the future.

Thank you.

China Is Exploiting Burma's Oil Supply and Threatening Its Environment

Marwaan Macan-Markar

Marwaan Macan-Markar is a reporter for Inter Press Service News Agency. In the following viewpoint, Macan-Markar observes that Burma's military dictatorship has allowed Chinese oil companies to explore and drill on Ramree Island in Burma without consulting the local peoples. This process has resulted in the destruction of rice fields and the exploitation of the natural landscape. Macan-Markar contends that human rights groups are concerned that projects like Ramree Island are funding Burma's military dictatorship, allowing them to gain an even tighter grip on power.

As you read, consider the following questions:

1. How many people live on Ramree Island, according to the author?
2. According to the human rights group EarthRights International, sixty-nine Chinese companies are involved in how many oil, gas, and hydropower projects in Burma?
3. As stated in the viewpoint, Burma was expected to earn how much from the export of gas in 2008?

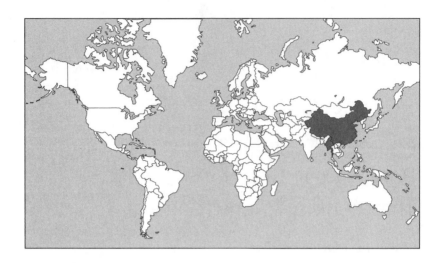

The largest island off Burma's west coast is emerging as another frontier for China's expanding plans to extract the rich oil and gas reserves of military-ruled Burma.

Initial explorations by a consortium, led by China National Offshore Oil Corporation (CNOOC), has left a deep scar on Ramree Island, which is twice the size of Singapore and home to about 400,000 people. "They have destroyed rice fields and plantations when conducting the seismic surveys and mining the island in search of oil," says Jockai Khaing, director of Arakan Oil Watch (AOW), an environmental group made up of Burmese living in exile.

"The local communities have been directly and indirectly affected," he said during an IPS [Inter Press Service, a global news agency] interview. "Hundreds of people have been forced to relocate as a result of the drilling conducted near their communities. The locals hate the Chinese; their world has become crazy after the Chinese arrived."

Concerns Are Increasing

CNOOC has been pushing ahead with its work since early 2005, with no attempt to consult the local residents and showing little regard to such notions as corporate social responsibility, adds Jockai. The Chinese company, which is listed on the New York and the Hong Kong stock exchanges, has "not conducted the required environmental impact assessments and social impact assessments that are recognised internationally as a must before exploration work begins."

To dispose the waste from its drilling sites, "CNOOC workers dug shallow canals designed to carry the (toxic) 'drilling mud,' or wastewater containing oil, away from the drilling sites and into Chaing Wa Creek, which curves past several local farms before flowing into the Bay of Bengal," states a report by AOW, released in mid-October [2008]. "This arbitrary disposal can make soil in surrounding areas unsuitable for plant growth by reducing the availability of nutrients or by increasing toxic contents in the soil."

"There are no rules and regulations for Chinese companies to follow in Burma."

Concerns about the cost of letting China tighten its grip on the natural resources in Burma (or Myanmar) has also been expressed by other groups, like EarthRights International (ERI), a U.S.-based group championing human rights. There are 69 Chinese companies involved in 90 "completed, current and planned projects" in the oil, gas and hydropower sectors in Burma, ERI revealed in a groundbreaking report released in late September [2007].

That number marks an over 200 percent increase in the number of Chinese energy developers thought to have had existed a year before. "Given what we know about development projects in Burma and the current situation, we're concerned about this marked increase in the number of the projects," the rights lobby stated in the report, *China in Burma: The Increasing Investment of Chinese Multinational Corporations in Burma's Hydropower, Oil and Natural Gas, and Mining Sectors.*

China's Investment in Burma

Introductory research conducted by the Burma Project over the past three months has found more than twenty-six Chinese multinational corporations (MNCs) involved in more than sixty-two hydropower, oil & gas, and mining projects in Burma. The projects vary from small dams completed in the past decade to planned dual oil and gas pipelines across Burma to Yunnan province announced this year [2007]. Detailed information about many of these investments is not made available to affected communities or the general public. . . .

Amidst the recent attention to China's moves to secure energy and resources throughout the world, Burma (also known as Myanmar) has too often been overlooked. The Southeast Asian country is rich in natural resources, from dense forests and untouched rivers to vast untapped reserves of minerals, oil, and natural gas. Ruled by one of the world's most notoriously brutal military regimes since 1962, Burma exemplifies the corruption, misuse of resources, and environmental devastation of the "resource curse."

EarthRights International, China in Burma, *September 2007.*

"China is using Burma's military dictatorship to its advantage as it goes in search of oil and gas. There are no rules and regulations for Chinese companies to follow in Burma," Ka Hsaw Wa, executive director of ERI, said in an IPS interview. "This will hurt the future of Burma."

China Is Set to Exploit Burma

Such criticisms come at a time when China has begun to show signs that the environmental cost of its projects abroad cannot be ignored. "The country lacked comprehensive environmental protection policies in its overseas projects, although investment had been expanding," states a report released in mid-September by the Chinese Academy for Environmental Planning (CAEP), according to the *China Daily* newspaper.

"China's overseas investment and aid mainly focus on exploring oil and other resources, processing and manufacturing, and construction in African and Southeast Asian countries," the English-language daily added. "Without proper management, such projects are likely to cause environmental problems, the (CAEP) report said."

Burma, in fact, will prove to be an ideal testing ground, given that China emerged as the military-ruled country's biggest investor in the country's power sector. The money flowing in from such foreign direct investments and the sale of gas has helped to prop up a junta [military ruling force] notorious for suppressing its people through many forms of abuse.

In 2006, the junta earned an estimated 2.16 billion U.S. dollars from sales of natural gas to Thailand, which accounts for close to half of Burma's export earnings and is the single largest source of foreign earnings. In 2008, Burma is expected to earn 3.5 billion U.S. dollars from export of gas, according to one estimate.

But little of these benefits trickled down to the country's beleaguered people. Consequently, Burma ranks as one of the world's least developed countries. And having an abundance of natural resources has not improved the power supply in the country for the people either. Regular blackouts are frequent in Rangoon, the former capital, and elsewhere.

The junta has profited in other ways, too, from China's energy interest in Burma. "Beijing has come to the junta's rescue and protects it from criticism at international forums like the UN [United Nations] Security Council," says Win Min, a Burmese national security expert teaching at a university in northern Thailand. "A strong relationship of mutual benefit has developed since 1988."

In exchange for letting Chinese companies exploit its natural resources, the Burmese dictatorship has gotten military hardware from Beijing. They range from fighter jets and armored carriers to small weapons, Win Min told IPS. "The junta will open the country to China because the military regime needs Beijing more than the other way around."

Periodical Bibliography

The following articles have been selected to supplement the diverse views presented in this chapter.

Tamsin Carlisle	"OPEC and IEA Singing off the Same Hymn Sheet," *National*, September 14, 2009.
Yemris Fointuna	"West Timor Sea 'Contaminated' by Oil Spill," *Jakarta Post*, October 29, 2009.
Lorrie Goldstein	"Oilsands a Topic for Adults Only," *Winnipeg Sun*, September 21, 2009.
Stephen Hesse	"Addiction Rages Blindly On," *Japan Times*, April 10, 2003.
Jeroen Kuiper	"Venezuela's Environment under Stress," Venezuelanalysis.com, March 1, 2005.
David Kulakofsky and Farzad Tahmourpour	"Cementing Solutions Help Protect the Environment," *E&P*, June 1, 2009.
Judy Maksoud	"Can the Impact of Drilling on the Environment Be Minimized with New Technology?" *E&P*, March 2, 2009.
Toni O'Loughlin	"Australian Oil Spill 'Contaminating One of the World's Richest Marine Wildernesses,'" *Guardian*, October 23, 2009.
Ed Pilkington	"U.S. Gives Shell Green Light for Offshore Oil Drilling in the Arctic," *Guardian*, October 20, 2009.
Ian Sample	"Amazon Threatened by New Oil and Gas Exploration," *Mail & Guardian Online*, August 13, 2008.
Ben Schiller	"China's African Encounter," *China Dialogue*, November 6, 2006.
John Vidal	"Canada Counts Its Dirty Oil Rush Costs," *Mail & Guardian Online*, July 24, 2008.

CHAPTER 3

Oil and Politics

Global Democracy and Oil

William Rees-Mogg

William Rees-Mogg is a respected columnist for the Times, *a daily newspaper published in the United Kingdom. In the following viewpoint, he argues that the discernible shift of the global economy from mature to emerging countries signals that oil-rich countries wield even more power as they control the flow of oil. That means leaders, he contends, do not have to answer to the people as long as they are being financed by oil.*

As you read, consider the following questions:

1. Who is Mahmoud Ahmadinejad, as stated in the viewpoint?
2. According to the author, how far did oil prices fall at the beginning of the global recession?
3. According to economists, what will the price of oil reach in 2010?

Dictatorships, as well as democracies, depend on money, although North Korea and Zimbabwe would like to prove the contrary. Dictators have their own constituencies and their constituencies have their own costs.

The victory of [Iranian president] Mahmoud Ahmadinejad may have been fraudulent; it is certainly bad news for the

Iranian people and the world. It means that the theocratic dictatorship of Iran will not benefit even from the modest reforms promised by [defeated candidate] Mir-Hossein Mousavi. The result will alienate the young urban middle class, particularly women. It will do nothing but damage to Iran's foreign relations.

It would be pleasant to suppose that the underlying trends of the economy would bring down this oppressive regime.

Global Oil Market Transformation

President Ahmadinejad is a dangerous populist who prides himself on his own ignorance, particularly of economics. He once said that he prayed to God that he would never know anything about economics because he regarded the whole subject as "a tool of Western imperialism". His prayer seems to have been answered; in 2007 he had to introduce petrol [gasoline] rationing in a leading oil-producing country.

Iran is primarily an oil economy; the global oil market is in the middle of an economic transformation.

The price of oil has been extraordinarily volatile. At the beginning of the recession it fell by about 80 per cent as world expectations were lowered. In the past six months [December–June 2009], the price has recovered by about 100 per cent, taking oil back to $70 a barrel.

These price gyrations need to be explained, particularly the strength of the price recovery in 2009; the recession may have reached bottom but it has certainly not reached this level of recovery.

Power Shift

Part of the explanation is the shift of the global economy from mature to emerging countries, particularly to the four biggest emerging markets of Brazil, Russia, India and China, the so-called BRIC countries, which are holding their own economic summit in Yekaterinburg [Russia] this week.

In coming years BRIC is expected to soar above the United States and Europe; China alone will catch up with the United States in five to ten years' time. The big emerging countries have continued to increase their demand for oil, even during the recession.

The swing of effective demand to the emerging countries is not in dispute, but there are different views about an even greater shift in the oil market, so-called "peak oil". That is the point in time when flows of new production are fully cancelled out by declines in existing production. That does not mean that oil is running out; but it does mean that demand will outstrip new supply, as has happened in the North Sea and North America. This time it will be a universal shortfall.

Oil Market Forecasts

Many experts believe that the recession has indeed passed its low point; in that case demand for oil will recover in the countries worst hit, but will also continue to increase in the emerging countries, particularly the BRIC countries. Much of the discussion in Yekaterinburg will centre on the future of oil supplies and particularly on the possible diversion of Russian oil from Europe to China.

If the peak oil theory does prove correct, the present recovery in prices will only be the beginning. Those oil economists who accept the peak oil argument tend to expect the price to reach $150 a barrel, probably in 2010.

"It is only too clear that most politicians are still living in the 20th-century world, the world in which they grew up."

This might be accompanied by a rise in the gold price above $1,000 an ounce. Oil and gold prices tend to move together, and the emerging countries have larger dollar reserves

Oil Reserves by Country

Rank	Countries	Amount
#1	Saudi Arabia:	262,700,000,000 barrels
#2	Canada:	178,900,000,000 barrels
#3	Iran:	133,300,000,000 barrels
#4	Iraq:	112,500,000,000 barrels
#5	United Arab Emirates:	97,800,000,000 barrels
#6	Kuwait:	96,500,000,000 barrels
#7	Venezuela:	75,590,000,000 barrels
#8	Russia:	69,000,000,000 barrels
#9	Libya:	40,000,000,000 barrels
#10	Nigeria:	36,000,000,000 barrels
#11	Mexico:	33,310,000,000 barrels
#12	Kazakhstan:	26,000,000,000 barrels
#13	Angola:	25,000,000,000 barrels
#14	United States:	22,450,000,000 barrels
#15	China:	18,260,000,000 barrels
#16	Qatar:	16,000,000,000 barrels
#17	Brazil:	15,120,000,000 barrels
#18	Algeria:	12,460,000,000 barrels
#19	Norway:	9,859,000,000 barrels
#20	Oman:	6,100,000,000 barrels
#21	India:	5,700,000,000 barrels
#22	Indonesia:	4,600,000,000 barrels
#23	Ecuador:	4,512,000,000 barrels
#24	United Kingdom:	4,500,000,000 barrels
#25	Yemen:	4,370,000,000 barrels
#26	Australia:	3,664,000,000 barrels

TAKEN FROM: *NationMaster.com*, 2009.

than they would altogether like. Gold is the one real alternative to paper currencies as a reserve asset.

The old assumptions are being undermined. It is only too clear that most politicians are still living in the 20th-century world, the world in which they grew up. The peak oil market may already have been reached, but in any case it will be reached eventually. The only question is when. Power is passing from the northwest to the southeast, from the United States to China.

Democracy Is Scarce in Oil-Rich Regions

Europe and the euro are very different from what they were. The euro is an oil-poor currency; oil-rich emerging currencies have the edge. Unfortunately, the natural logic of liberal democracy does not fit the natural logic of the oil market. Countries tend to become more liberal when the people are rich and the state is poor.

In 1215 King John was weak and he had to make concessions to the barons. That was how England got Magna Carta. When the state becomes independently wealthy, as the oil states now are, they do not have to persuade their people, because they can rely on external income. Unfortunately, there is a global shift of wealth in favour of the oil countries, few of which are democracies. Even in Russia one can see that the post-Communist administrations have been more or less authoritarian according to the price of oil. Boris Yeltsin's liberalism was a response to a fall in the oil price; Vladimir Putin's authoritarianism is equally a response to a high oil price, which has boosted his revenues. The Iranian dictatorship has increasing revenue from oil.

President Ahmadinejad does not have to worry too much about elections because he knows where his regime's money will be coming from. It will come from oil and not from the people—and the price will continue to rise. As an economist, he is not as stupid as he makes out.

Nigeria Deals with Political Havoc Caused by Oil Companies

Anup Shah

Anup Shah is a reporter for Global Issues. *In the following viewpoint, he reviews what he sees as heavy-handed and immoral activities taken against Nigerian citizens and protestors by large, transnational oil companies doing business in the Niger Delta. Shah charges that these companies support repressive and corrupt dictatorships in order to exploit Nigeria's rich oil reserves and often endanger the environment in the process.*

As you read, consider the following questions:

1. What has Human Rights Watch said about the role of multinational oil companies in crackdowns on protestors in the Niger Delta?

2. According to the author, what kind of environmental damage do environmentalists accuse multinational oil companies of in the Niger Delta region?

3. According to the study "Peace and Security in the Niger Delta," what are some of the accusations against Shell and its activities in Nigeria?

The Niger Delta in Nigeria has been the attention of environmentalists, human rights activists and fair trade advocates around the world. The trial and hanging of environmen-

Anup Shah, "Nigeria and Oil," *Global Issues*, July 3, 2004. Reproduced by permission.

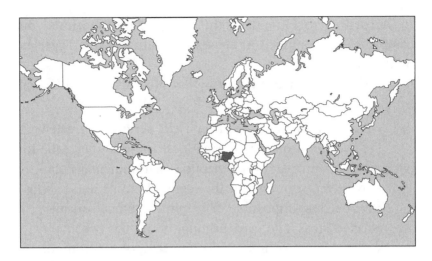

talist Ken Saro-Wiwa and eight other members of the Ogoni ethnic minority made worldwide attention. So too did the nonviolent protests of the Ogoni people. The activities of large oil corporations such as Mobil, Chevron, Shell, Elf [Aquitaine, currently known as Total], Agip, etc., have raised many concerns and criticisms.

A series of repressive and corrupt governments in Nigeria have been supported and maintained by Western governments and oil corporations, keen on benefiting from the fossil fuels that can be exploited. As people and transnational oil corporations have been fighting over this "dark nectar" in the delta region, immense poverty and environmental destruction have resulted.

Abuses Abound

The Ogoni, Ijaw and other people in the Niger Delta, those who have been worse affected for decades, have been trying to stand up for themselves, their environment and their basic human and economic rights. The Nigerian government and the oil companies have responded by harshly cracking down on protestors. Shell, for example, has even been criticized for trying to divide communities by paying off some members to disrupt nonviolent protests.

According to Human Rights Watch, "multinational oil companies are complicit in abuses committed by the Nigerian military and police."

An investigation and report by Essential Action and Global Exchange found that:

1. Oil corporations in the Niger Delta seriously threaten the livelihood of neighboring local communities. Due to the many forms of oil-generated environmental pollution evident throughout the region, farming and fishing have become impossible or extremely difficult in oil-affected areas, and even drinking water has become scarce. Malnourishment and disease appear common.

2. The presence of multinational oil companies has had additional adverse effects on the local economy and society, including loss of property, price inflation, prostitution, and irresponsible fathering by expatriate oil workers.

3. Organized protest and activism by affected communities regularly meet with military repression, sometimes ending in the loss of life. In some cases military forces have been summoned and assisted by oil companies.

4. Reporting on the situation is extremely difficult, due to the existence of physical and legal constraints to free passage and free circulation of information. Similar constraints discourage grassroots activism.

Oil Companies Influence Government Reactions

While the story told to consumers of Nigerian crude in the United States and the European Union—via ad campaigns and other public relations efforts—is that oil companies are a positive force in Nigeria, providing much-needed economic development resources, the reality that confronted our delegation was quite the opposite. Our delegates observed almost every large multinational oil company operating in the Niger Delta employing inadequate environmental standards, public health standards, human rights standards, and relations with affected communities. These corporations' acts of charity and development are slaps in the face of those they claim to be helping. Far from being a positive force, these oil companies act as a destabilizing force, pitting one community against another, and acting as a catalyst—together with the military with whom they work closely—to some of the violence racking the region today.

> —*Oil for Nothing: Multinational Corporations, Environmental Destruction, Death and Impunity in the Niger Delta, Essential Action and Global Exchange, January 25, 2000*

There have been many clear examples of corporate influence in the Nigerian military repressing the protestors. The military have been accused of thousands of killings, house/village burnings, intimidating people, torture and so on. From Shell's involvement in the killing of Ken Saro-Wiwa to Chevron-marked helicopters carrying Nigerian military that opened fire upon protestors, the corporations are facing harsh criticisms for the way they have been handling (or encouraging) the situation.

Criticisms abound about the way the oil companies have neglected the surrounding environment and health of the local communities. The Niger Delta is the richest area of biodiversity in Nigeria, but regular oil spills that are not cleaned up, blatant dumping of industrial waste and promises of development projects which are not followed through, have all added to the increasing environmental and health problems.

The latest government has tried to be more democratic and open, which provides hope. However, there are still a number of problems to be solved, including corruption and religious tensions between Muslims and Christians. There were riots and killings, for example, at Muslim calls for imposition of Sharia, Islamic criminal law.

Oil and the Nigerian People

The oil-rich Niger Delta region of southern Nigeria has seen escalating conflict and violence in the last two decades. Oil revenues account for over 98 per cent of Nigeria's foreign exchange earnings. However, little of this wealth is distributed within the Niger Delta, or to the Nigerian people as a whole. Economic and social rights, such as the right to health and the right to an adequate standard of living, remain unfulfilled for many Nigerians.

Amnesty International,
"Nigeria: Oil, Poverty and Violence," August 2006.

"Criticisms abound about the way oil companies have neglected the surrounding environment and health of the local communities."

The Situation Has Not Improved

Most of the above was written in 2000. Well, into 2004, things have generally not improved. For example, the *International Herald Tribune* reports on a study titled "Peace and Security in the Niger Delta" where amongst other things, the following was noted:

- Shell companies have worsened fighting in the Niger Delta through payments for land use, environmental damage, corruption of company employees and reliance on Nigerian security forces.

- The action of Shell companies and their staff creates, feeds into, or exacerbates conflict.

- Violence in the Niger Delta kills some 1,000 people each year, on par with conflicts in Chechnya and Colombia

- With over 50 years of presence in Nigeria, it is reasonable to say that the Shell companies in Nigeria have become an integral part of the Niger Delta conflict.

In response to this, Shell had said that it remained "committed to corporate social responsibility", whereas the report was saying that it had not acted that way! Furthermore Shell made a weak concession and recognized that its development activities in the past "may have been less than perfect." Compare this to the accusation from the report of being part of the conflict for so long and even making things worse, this admission can be regarded as very weak. To the credit of Shell, this December 2003 report was actually commissioned by it. Usually if people are found to be complicit in acts of crime, etc., then some sort of criminal justice is expected. One doesn't expect Shell to have a criminal case of any sort brought against it. The *Tribune* article didn't even raise this as an issue.

Angola Learns Valuable Lessons About Oil

Polly Ng and Philippe Le Billon

Philippe Le Billon is an assistant professor at the University of British Columbia and the Liu Institute for Global Issues. Polly Ng is a student. In the following viewpoint, they explore the example of Angola to illuminate the point that oil wealth can often be a blessing and a curse, causing many political and economic problems. Ng and Le Billon contend that Angola's struggles can provide valuable lessons for the oil-rich country of Sudan.

As you read, consider the following questions:

1. How long was Angola's civil war, as stated in the viewpoint?
2. According to the authors, in the five years since the end of the civil war, what happened to Angola's annual oil revenues?
3. Where do the authors say Angola ranks among forty countries in a survey of government transparency?

Oil wealth has long proved an ambivalent asset for producing countries. If oil wealth can provide the means of improving the lives of citizens, and fast-track recovery from

Polly Ng and Philippe Le Billon, "'Post-Conflict' Oil Governance: Lessons from Angola?" *DIIS Report: Oil Development in Africa: Lessons for Sudan After the Comprehensive Peace Agreement, 2007:8*, Copenhagen: DIIS–Danish Institute for International Studies, 2007. © Copenhagen 2007 Danish Institute for International Studies, DIIS. Reproduced by permission of DIIS; Editor, Luke Patey.

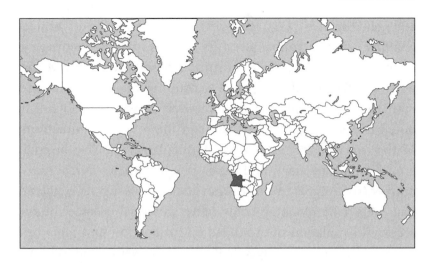

deadly conflicts, the recent literature has demonstrated how oil dependence can prove counterproductive to economic development and social well-being. Oil dependence is also associated with poor governance and corruption, as guaranteed resource revenues for the state create a democratic deficit. There is also good evidence that oil dependence contributes to armed conflict, as different groups struggle to control territories where resources are located. This so-called 'resource curse' is not inevitable, however. Under the right conditions, revenues generated by natural resources, including oil, present enormous opportunities, and particularly so for poor countries emerging from decades of conflicts like Angola and Sudan.

Peace Brings Investment

In February 2002, Angolan troops killed UNITA's [National Union for the Total Independence of Angola] leader, Jonas Savimbi, putting an end to 27 years of civil war. This military victory, and the subsequent amnesty and peace agreement with UNITA troops on 5 April 2002 allowed the government to claim that the country had finally made a durable transition to peace after two failed peace agreements in 1991 and

1994. In the five years following the termination of armed conflict, Angola's annual gross oil revenues nearly quadrupled from US$8 to US$30 billion. Although some of this revenue went to foreign oil companies recouping major new investments (i.e., 'cost oil'), this unprecedented wealth held much potential for consolidating peace and improving the situations of the overwhelming majority of Angolans, who live in poverty. Fiscal, budgetary, and development policies by the government of Angola are of course key to realising such potential, even if the country holds much potential outside the oil sector. A simulation of expanded oil production in Angola between 2001 and 2010 suggests that if policies are right, oil revenues have the ability to significantly reduce poverty levels by 2010. To improve the well-being of the poor, rather than simply promote economic growth, such policies need to specifically target the poor and seek to reduce inequalities through income redistribution, the improvement of social services and infrastructures, as well as reviving the agricultural and industrial sectors. Development economist Paul Collier articulates in more details the priority actions that Angola should take, so that in 30 years its situation resembles more the track followed by Malaysia, rather than that of Nigeria.

Despite continued conflict in Darfur and renewed uncertainty in the south, opportunities are also currently available for Sudan, with the cessation of its long and intractable civil war in the south under the 2005 Comprehensive Peace Agreement and the rapid development of its oil sector since 1999. This [viewpoint] examines the situation of oil governance in Angola prior to and after the termination of its civil war in 2002 in order to draw observations that may be of some relevance for the Sudan. Not all 'lessons' from Angola will be applicable to Sudan, as many factors distinguish the two countries, but in both cases a fundamental challenge remains: the governance of the oil sector for sustainable peace and the betterment of their people. . . .

Angola's Transition to "Peace"

Angola's decades-long civil war came to an end with the signing of the 'Memorandum of Understanding [Addendum to the Lusaka Protocol] for the Cessation of Hostilities and the Resolution of the Outstanding Military Issues Under the Lusaka Protocol' on 4 April 2002 by the military leaders of the FAA [Angolan Armed Forces] and UNITA. The conclusion of the conflict was the result of the MPLA's [Popular Movement for the Liberation of Angola] definitive military victory over UNITA, which produced a government-driven end to armed hostilities that excluded all political and social stakeholders other than the two sides of the conflict and left unaddressed important considerations for effective change. . . .

"Oil revenues have the ability to significantly reduce poverty levels."

Oil, Peace and Prosperity?

The preservation and consolidation of the power of the MPLA party through the military peace established by the government's definitive military victory and its skilful manoeuvres in the . . . peace process has meant that the government has had little incentive and has therefore taken little action to change its method of oil governance despite the opportunities for overcoming the legacies of civil war presented by rapid expansion of oil production and rising oil revenues.

There have been no legislative changes regarding allocation of oil revenues and, although some positive changes have been made, the problems of government misallocation of oil rents, the lack of transparency, and pervasive corruption stemming from poor governance persist in the post-war period and undermine the development of democratic peace and the improvement of the lives of Angolans. Defence and security expenditures continue to claim a portion of oil revenues that is disturbingly high for peacetime. The proportion of total expenditures captured by defence and public order rose to 13.8 percent in 2003, dropping slightly to 12.5 percent in 2004. Such priorities threaten to crowd out much-needed spending on the provision of elementary services to the public and infrastructure reconstruction.

Call for Transparency

The government maintains its reliance on costly oil-backed loans from commercial banks to pay back its public external debt, which currently amounts to over $2 billion excluding late interest. A comprehensive report released in January 2004 by Human Rights Watch (HRW), including an IMF-requested [International Monetary Fund-requested] 'oil diagnostic study,' points to continuing deficiencies in transparency in oil governance and concludes that "[t]he Angolan government has consistently mismanaged its substantial oil revenues and, despite rhetorical comments, has yet to demonstrate a meaningful commitment to reform." . . . The government does not sufficiently report how it spends its oil revenues, a critical component especially since revenues have been increasing due to new oil bonus payments, generous loans from China, and buoyant oil prices. Despite many promises made to the IMF, there is still a lack of budgetary transparency, with Angola ranking as the second least transparent government in a survey of 40 countries. Angola also remains among the world's most corrupt countries, even if its ranking improved from 98th out of 102 countries . . . in 2002, to 142nd out of 163 in 2006 . . . according to Transparency International's Corruption Perceptions Index. Hence, the IMF and other lending institutions maintain wariness towards the Angolan government and demand that greater transparency in revenues and expenditures is needed before they are willing to extend formal lending programs to the country.

Corruption continues to be a serious problem, with recent scandals evidencing the prevalence of corruption. In 2003, the Angolan government installed Pierre Falcone as its representative to UNESCO [United Nations Educational, Scientific and Cultural Organization] so that he could escape French judicial authorities for his involvement in arms trafficking in exchange for oil in 1993. The Angolan National Police arrested more than 100 protestors in November 2005 when they charged the government with misspending billions of public dollars. Though most were released within 24 hours, 27 individuals, who were identified as members of the opposition Party for Progress were detained and some reported mistreatment by the police. The incident prompted Arvind Ganesan, director of HRW's business and human rights program, to state that, "[t]he Angolan government should tackle corruption and mismanagement, not arrest those who publicise the problems. Arresting critics shows the government isn't serious about reforms to improve transparency and curb corruption."

Few Changes in Angola

The conclusion of four decades of armed conflict in 2002 has also brought few changes to Angola's political regime and governance. Despite the message of forgiveness, national reconciliation, and reconstruction and the promise of free elections given by President [José Eduardo] dos Santos before the memorandum signing ceremony, military peace has allowed the MPLA party to effectively continue single-party politics, with little room for political opposition and effective challenging of autocratic structures and further hindering the consolidation of peace. . . .

Freedom of expression, association, and assembly remains feeble. Political opponents suffer violence from the police, military, the [International] Civil Defence Organisation, and MPLA allies. The government limits spaces and opportunities

Sudan Oil Fields and Pipeline

TAKEN FROM: http://southsudanfriends.org.

for democracy by tightly controlling state-owned media, frequently omitting critical voices and arguments, and prohibiting the Catholic broadcasting station, Rádio Ecclesia, from broadening its signal outside of the capital city. . . . Poverty remains extreme; with 2004 data ranking Angola 79th of 102 developing countries, according to UNDP's [United Nations Development Programme's] Human Development Index, and 70 percent of the population living on less than a dollar a day. . . .

Lessons from Angola?

The evolution of the Angolan oil sector in relation to 'post-conflict' peace-building suggests that high income has promoted the preexisting political status quo that maintained in place the largely authoritarian regime. Not only did the Angolan government 'win' the war against UNITA (and corner key FLEC [guerrilla and political movement] factions), but its growing geostrategic and commercial importance as well as its high economic growth are making it relatively immune to both external and domestic political opposition. At the external level, the Angolan government has been able to convince foreign governments to work in 'partnership' with it. At the domestic level, the government has been able to 'purchase' or 'cow' political opposition in the face of rapidly rising inequalities and postponed general elections. The result has been 're-gime stability' but a fragile peace. Even though rising oil revenues could (and should) greatly improve social conditions, the shortage of transparency in government practices and the lack of accountability created by both the democratic deficit and by the government's restrictions on political opposition and criticism mean that oil rent continues to benefit few in Angolan society.

"Even though rising oil revenues could (and should) greatly improve social conditions ... oil rent continues to benefit few in Angolan society."

Oil has so far contributed to peace-building through post-conflict reconstruction and development-oriented initiatives. Although official development aid to Angola increased sharply in 2004, many Western donors have been reluctant to provide unconditional support given the level of revenues collected by the government and its relative lack of progress on key governance issues. As a result, domestic revenues (as well as grants and loans from less-demanding donors, notably China and to some extent the United States and Portugal) have addressed demobilisation efforts and some of the massive needs of the population. Oil revenues have helped to finance the necessary processes of demobilisation, disarmament and reintegration, though progress in these areas remains slow and ongoing. Social spending has improved significantly but not by the leaps and bounds that it should, given the abundance of oil revenue.

"There are strong linkages between political governance and oil governance."

There may be some relevant insights for the situation in Sudan:

- Oil revenues tend to maintain the power of former elites. It is thus important to integrate reforms at an early stage before leverage is further undermined and vested interests consolidated.

- The nature of conflict termination is influential on how oil governance and political regime may affect the aftermath of civil war. It is thus important to articulate a negotiated settlement with broader reforms.

- There are strong linkages between political governance and oil governance. Political opening and power sharing between different groups in society (e.g., a diversity of political parties, media watchdogs, civil society organisations, and members of the public) as well as mechanisms to hold the government transparent and accountable for responsible expenditure for oil revenue can increase regime legitimacy and progressive reforms, notably through a better allocation of oil revenues. This allocation should neither focus on a 'populist' agenda of poverty alleviation reminiscent of selective patronage politics; nor should it concentrate on an 'elitist' agenda of economic modernisation characterised by crony capitalism. Rather, this allocation should seek to address the immediate needs of population, while aiming for a genuine opening of the economy and society in general.

Sudan's Oil Industry Causes Harm

Ruth West

Ruth West is a contributor to the New Statesman, *Britain's current affairs and politics magazine. In the following viewpoint, Ruth West asserts that Sudan's oil industry has been used to finance a civil war between the Muslim northern region, where the government is located, and the Christian/African southern region of Sudan, where the oil is located. Foreign investment in Sudan's oil industry pays the government for protection from attacks by those in the south. The government uses this investment money to buy weapons to exterminate its enemies in the south.*

As you read, consider the following questions:

1. What is the SPLA?
2. What does Amnesty International believe about the situation in Sudan?
3. Who is Jim Buckee, and what role has his company played in Sudan?

Sudan may be desperately poor, but it does have oil. The country lacks the necessary technology to exploit its sought-after resource, and has invited foreign companies to do so. Such arrangements have become a model for "develop-

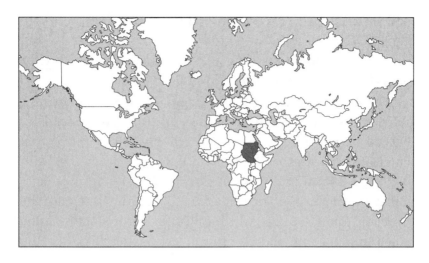

ment": oil companies can pay their shareholders, build schools and hospitals for the local communities, and the host country grows richer.

But with oil, things are never so straightforward. This is especially true of Sudan, the largest country in Africa. It has been torn by a stop-and-start civil war since independence from Britain in 1956; the oil is in the mainly Christian and African south, where the many factions of the Sudan People's Liberation Army (SPLA) operate; the government, the SPLA's foe, is in the north, which is mainly Muslim and Arab.

The government receives US$1m a day in royalties from foreign oil companies—and spends US$1m a day on bombs and troops directed against the "rebels" in the south. Since 1956, an estimated two million Sudanese have been killed, more than five million have been displaced internally, and one million are now in exile.

Human rights reports agree: the war was partly started by oil exploitation. (It was presaged by the killing of three Chevron oil workers in 1984; the US company then pulled out.) The war escalated with the return of the foreign oil companies in 1997; the western companies sought government protection from the SPLA rebels who controlled much of the oil-rich land in the south. The government was only too happy to comply. Its "protection" of petroleum concession areas allowed for the looting and burning of villages and crops; and for rape, abduction and torture.

Thanks to this foreign investment, the government now has a military victory in its sights. Oil production stands at 200,000 barrels a day, and may reach 400,000 by 2005; estimates of defence expenditure have thus risen from US$373m in 1998 to $425m in 2000. Not surprisingly, last April, Sudan's president, Omar Hassan el-Bashir, turned down a ceasefire proposal from the SPLA, which called for oil production to be halted until a comprehensive peace deal was reached.

"Human rights reports agree: the war was partly started by oil exploitation."

Defenders of the Sudanese government and the oil companies claim that there is no hard evidence to link oil revenues with military expenditure. Yet Amnesty International is in no doubt that "by turning a blind eye, in the name of security, to the violations committed by government forces and troops allied to them, [the oil firms] indirectly contribute to violations continuing".

One of the main oil companies in Sudan is Talisman Energy Inc, based in Calgary, Canada. When its CEO and president, Dr Jim Buckee, was challenged by human rights organisations at the firm's annual general meeting last May, he defended its record: "We share the same values as you do. . . . we are doing good in Sudan." Yes, Talisman has spent C$lm ([pounds sterling]435,000) on 15 development projects, including clinics, schools and wells. The problem is that they are mainly in garrison towns, and thus inaccessible to the rural people who need them.

Now Talisman faces a $1bn class-action suit, brought against the company by two US lawyers. The complaint was filed in New York on 8 November last year on behalf of four southern Sudanese people. But as Carey D'Avino, one of the prosecuting lawyers, told me: "We are seeking compensation for anyone suffering injuries and losses because of Talisman in or within 50 miles of the company's concession area in the Sudan."

"But 11 September changed all that. US diplomats at the UN sat by as sanctions against Sudan were lifted in exchange for information on terrorists."

In 1996, the US supported United Nations sanctions against Sudan, and in 1997 it imposed sanctions of its own, prohibiting companies on the New York Stock Exchange from doing business there. Yet when major oil companies began showing an interest in Sudan, they were exempted from the sanctions. The US also sent money and supplies to the SPLA; under the Clinton administration, the USAID development agency financed a grant programme to the south of $10m to support the "liberation struggle". Under George W. Bush, food aid has been sent directly to the north for the first time in ten years. A peace envoy, Senator John Danforth, was appointed in September. Three months earlier, the House of Representatives had passed the Sudan Peace Act (now before a joint House and Senate committee, where Wall Street lobbyists are confident it will languish); this authorised a further $10m for the southern rebels and included an amendment to prohibit foreign oil companies operating in Sudan from being listed on any US stock exchange.

But 11 September changed all that. US diplomats at the UN sat by as sanctions against Sudan were lifted in exchange for information on terrorists. As Richard Boucher, the State Department spokesman, said: "We're not going to say, 'We won't accept your information on terrorism unless you stop bombing civilians.'" No matter that Osama Bin Laden lived in

Sudan for five years in the 1990s and still has major business interests there in banking, construction and agriculture; or that Sudan is home to terrorist training camps and serves as a safe haven for Islamic Jihad and Hamas.

In November, US sanctions were renewed for another year and Danforth was back, calling on the government of Sudan and the SPLA to make progress by mid-January, otherwise "I'm simply going to report to the president that we tried, we did our best and that there is no further useful role the United States can play".

The Sudanese government's determination to exterminate its enemies in the south is fuelled by revenues from foreign oil firms. These companies should be held accountable for human rights abuses carried out because of their activities. The only way to do this is to hit them where it hurts, by imposing tough new regulations on their involvement in developing countries.

São Tomé and Príncipe Aim to Develop an Oil Industry and Protect Quality of Life

Integrated Regional Information Networks (IRIN)

Integrated Regional Information Networks (IRIN) is a news agency of the United Nations Office for the Coordination of Humanitarian Affairs. In the following viewpoint, IRIN reports that oil exploration has turned up billions of gallons of oil under the islands of São Tomé and Príncipe. This has raised concerns about the effects oil wealth will have on the economic, political, and social life of the small, peaceful islands.

As you read, consider the following questions:

1. What is São Tomé's relationship with Nigeria, according to the author?
2. According to the viewpoint, what have been some of the repercussions of São Tomé's newfound oil wealth?
3. How much have oil companies paid out to São Tomé for the right to look for oil, according to IRIN?

These sleepy twin islands poking out from the depths of the Atlantic Ocean are among the most peaceful places on earth. Now, with geological surveys suggesting that the islands could be sitting on billions of barrels of oil and, with a popu-

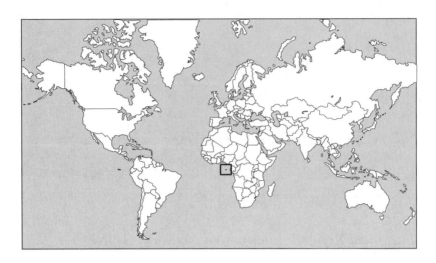

lation of less than 150,000, every man, woman and child on the islands could, in theory, become millionaires.

Some of the world's biggest oil companies have already paid hundreds of millions of dollars for the right to drill oil in the surrounding waters. However, experts on the effects of sudden resource wealth in poor countries are sounding the alarm that São Tomé and Príncipe could destabilize and even collapse.

"The production of natural resources is liable to give rise to various types of political frustrations within a country." That is the view of such leading economists as Jeffrey D. Sachs, and Nobel Prize winner Joseph E. Stiglitz, writing together with political scientist Macartan Humphreys in *Escaping the Resource Curse*, a book to be released by Columbia University Press in June 2007.

"São Tomé and Príncipe could destabilise and even collapse."

In the introduction, Humphreys, Sachs, and Stiglitz warn that, "resource-rich countries grew less rapidly than resource-poor countries during the last quarter of the twentieth century." Plus, they said, "[research suggests] a strong association between resource wealth and the likelihood of weak democratic development, corruption, and civil war."

Yet researchers specialized on São Tomé remain divided over whether it is going the same way. It does not have a history of social tensions and there has not been political bloodshed.

"I basically remain optimistic," said Gerhard Seibert, a researcher from the Lisbon-based Tropical Research Institute and author of a book on political and economic changes in the country since Portuguese rule ended in 1975. "I just don't think things will get as bad as in other oil-rich African countries."

Still, he and others express concerns about the corrupting influence of the nearby economic and military giant Nigeria, with which São Tomé has agreed to share its oil wealth.

Theory or Practice?

Crime remains low in the quaint seaside capital São Tomé (which carries the same name as the island), and where everyone seems to know each other. "There is more money floating around," said Martin Sandbu, a specialist in the political economy of natural resource wealth at the University of Pennsylvania's Wharton School of Business, who recently returned from the islands. "Although the divide between the rich and poor is also increasing," he added.

"For the general population, the economy is stagnating and people don't seem hopeful that the government is going to be able to do anything about it," he said.

For Seibert, the oil has clearly come with social, economic and political costs. Competition over the wealth risks is fracturing the government and exacerbating discontent within the country's tiny armed forces, he said. In January 2006, police revolted after the government failed to pay them their salaries, he noted. And in 2003, soldiers, led by Major Fernando Pereira, attempted a coup while President Fradique de Menezes was visiting Nigeria.

Pereira and his men stood down when Nigeria threatened to intervene.

Since then, there have been few other signs of trouble, even during three rounds of national elections in 2006, in which Nigeria provided campaign funds to many candidates, and there were widespread reports of vote buying.

The reelected government has insisted that it has seen what has happened to other oil-rich African countries and it is not going to make the same mistakes. "Here, oil receipts will benefit the whole population," its spokesman, Adelino Lucas, told IRIN [Integrated Regional Information Networks].

The government has been praised for a law passed in 2004 laying out how it must spend the revenue it gets from oil. The law's stated aim: "The elimination of poverty and the improvement of the quality of life of the São Toméan people to ensure a harmonious and integrated development of the country, and a fair sharing of the national wealth".

So Where's the Money?

So far, not a drop of the oil has been pumped out of São Tomé's waters. In May 2006, Chevron announced for the first time that it had struck oil, though it also said it would need to do more drilling to determine whether the discovery is commercially viable, and that would not start until the end of 2007.

Oil companies have, however, already paid out some $237 million for the right to look for the oil, although only a fraction of the money has gone to São Toméans.

One reason is that São Tomé agreed to share the wealth with Nigeria, taking only 40 percent. As Nigeria bore the initial cost of setting up the joint arrangement—which many experts said Nigeria inflated—São Tomé has had to use much of its oil money to pay Nigeria back.

The Danger of Oil Wealth

A decade ago, geologists found signs that one of Africa's least-known countries, the tiny island nation of São Tomé and Príncipe, might hold a king's ransom in oil.

The first drop of oil has yet to be produced. But these days, little São Tomé may have attracted ample supplies of something else, federal investigators suspect—oil-related corruption.

All of this might not seem unusual in Africa, where oil and corruption often go hand in hand. However, São Tomé, a former Portuguese colony off the coast of Nigeria, was supposed to be different. In recent years, a steady stream of activists like the Columbia University economist Jeffrey D. Sachs have gone there to try to make sure that any energy boom would benefit its 150,000 people, rather than politicians and companies.

"Oil can be a blessing or a bane for a country," Mr. Sachs said. "The theory was to help São Tomé avoid the resource curse."

Barry Meier and Jad Mouawad,
"No Oil Yet, but African Isle Finds Slippery Dealings,"
New York Times, July 2, 2007.

Yet, even out of the estimated US$80 million that Sandbu reckons the government has received, less than US$30 million has gone into government coffers, with the rest being invested in New York on interest-bearing securities. This was what Sachs and his team, along with the World Bank and IMF [International Monetary Fund], had called for. They said the government was not yet set up to use the money effectively, plus a sudden spike in spending in the country would exacerbate inflation which already stands at 20 percent.

Meanwhile most São Toméans want to see tangible benefits from the oil money, and that is one of the other many dilemmas for oil-rich countries, said Jenik Radon, the author of one of the chapters in *Escaping the Resource Curse*: "How can the challenge of rising expectations, desires, and demands be satisfied."

Radon also notes that when governments get revenue from oil companies, rather than by taxing their own citizens, they become less responsive to local concerns.

On the streets of São Tomé people are expressing frustration. "Politicians are all bad," said one young man who requested anonymity. "They only look after themselves with good cars and big houses. For the rest of us, we will continue to be poor," he said.

"When governments get revenue from oil companies . . . they become less responsive to local concerns."

Corruption or Ineptitude?

Jose Cardoso works in São Tomé for a coalition of NGOs [nongovernmental organizations] called Publish What You Pay. The coalition is pressing for transparency in the oil industry, although he said it is still too early to say whether the oil money is being misused. "We don't have access to data because the activities are very new," he said. But he added, "There is a possibility of irregularities, without a doubt."

For Sandbu, "The government is weak on laws and policies for awarding new contracts to oil companies, as well as on what to do about the bad agreements it made in the past," he said. Good laws on how the government spends its revenue are not much use if the revenue never gets into its coffers, he added.

The researchers have seen evidence of politicians making shady deals with oil companies for personal gain. Sandbu said the government has so far lost at least US$58 million because of bad oil deals, which he said is likely to be the tip of the iceberg.

But the question is whether the bad deals were a result of incompetence or corruption.

President de Menezes blames his predecessors for agreements made with questionable Nigerian and US-based companies, and he has since reneged on some of the deals. Yet in October [2006], the Norwegian watchdog NGO Norwatch released an investigation of agreements between the São Tomé government and a company called [Petroleum] Geo-Services (PGS) which said, "Political contacts all the way inside São Tomé's presidential family enabled the Norwegian seismic services company PGS [Petroleum Geo-Services] to obtain two lucrative agreements in 2001."

The company and the president have denied any wrongdoing, but as people's frustrations grow, appearances are what count. The former coup leader, Major Pereira, who has since been reinstated into the army, told IRIN, "We have seen corruption and all we want is to stop it."

Oil, Poverty, and Terrorism Are Linked Concerns

Mohamed Sid-Ahmed

Mohamed Sid-Ahmed is a prominent Egyptian political commentator. In the following viewpoint, he underscores the need to address poverty in the war against terror. Sid-Ahmed acknowledges that poverty and terrorism are inextricably linked, and unless the world formulates a way to evenly distribute wealth and opportunity, terrorism will exist and even flourish. Securing the global oil supply and putting oil revenues to good use are key parts of the fight.

As you read, consider the following questions:

1. What are the two categories of oil-producing states, according to the author?
2. What country is cited as the largest oil producer in the world?
3. What is the combined revenue of oil-producing countries per day, according to the viewpoint?

The Nobel Foundation's decision to award this year's [2005's] peace prize to the International Atomic [Energy] Agency and its director, Mohamed ElBaradei, highlights the importance of the energy sector in today's world. Despite the enormous effort put into the search for alternative sources of energy, most controversially nuclear, oil remains the principal source of energy worldwide. It also stands at the heart of many of the crisis situations threatening global stability. Indeed, it would be no exaggeration to say that solving the oil problem would help solve many other intricate problems as well.

With oil still the fuel that drives the global economy, the sudden unprecedented rise in oil prices, which experts predict will not go down in the foreseeable future, is a particularly disquieting development. Actually, the rise could be as much of a bane for the oil producers themselves as it is for the oil-importing countries. The proceeds of the first price hike in the 1970s did more to spread corruption and deepen social ills than promote development and growth. Will the tragedy be repeated this time around?

Two Categories of Oil-Producing Countries

Oil-producing states have been divided into two categories: states with small populations and huge oil reserves and states with large populations and oil reserves incommensurate with their high population density. The discrepancy between these two categories of states has been a permanent source of friction between them. The states with rich reserves and limited populations are tempted to keep the oil as long as possible under the ground, while the second category has no choice but to bow to heavy consumption demands at the expense of preserving their oil wealth.

In a category of its own is Saudi Arabia, the largest oil producer in the world. Though technically part of the first group of states, it is in fact under tremendous pressure to use up its oil reserves far more rapidly than is necessary to cover the needs of its population. Blurring as it does the lines of demarcation between the two categories, Saudi Arabia further complicates the already complex oil equation, multiplies the possible scenarios and was partly responsible in the 1970s and 1980s for the intensification of inter-Arab conflict and the collapse of oil prices.

Another special case is Iran. Once the second largest oil-producing country in the world, its known oil reserves have been severely depleted over the years. Still, it remains a major player in the oil market and its destabilisation is bound to impact negatively on the market. It is to nobody's advantage to expose Iran to turmoil and yet that seems to be what the Bush administration is trying to do. Its confrontation with Iran, part of the "axis of evil", is now limited to a war of words but things could turn ugly if the standoff over Iran's nuclear programme is not resolved.

Since 2000, oil prices have tripled and the combined revenues of oil-producing countries now stand at $2 billion a day. The average price of a barrel has risen from $20 to $60. In Saudi Arabia, which suffered from a sharp depreciation of its oil revenues throughout the 1990s, the price of oil has increased by 40 per cent. There has been a number of other positive developments. The last few years have seen petrodollars being invested in the oil-producing counties themselves rather than in foreign holdings and assets, as was the case up until the 1990s. In less than one year, funds once invested in the United States, Europe and Japan have helped revitalize the stock exchanges in many of the oil-producing countries. However, expectations have not been fulfilled on all fronts, with Russia unable to reestablish itself as the world's second superpower and Africa unable to achieve its takeoff.

"Fighting terrorism will not succeed as long as a shattering blow has not been delivered against poverty."

Addressing Poverty Is the Key

A tremendous amount of work still remains to be done. Millions of jobs will need to be created, especially in Africa and

"Boom or Bust," cartoon by Tim Cordell. Copyright © Tim Cordell and CartoonStock .com. Reproduction rights obtainable from www.CartoonStock.com.

the Middle East. Contrary to what happened under the first price surge, work is being done to build an infrastructure in a variety of fields such as roads, ports, communication and tourist facilities. When it comes to education and health, however, not enough is being done and the whole field has been left largely to initiatives by conservative Islamic groups.

The two scourges of our time, terrorism and poverty, are inextricably linked. Unless and until the world works out a fair distribution of wealth, the war against terrorism cannot succeed. We must declare war on poverty and take serious measures to eradicate it. This entails fighting corruption, waste and various forms of pollution, not only of nature, but also of societal values. The current surge in oil and gas prices must be put to good use to avoid a repeat performance of what happened with the first oil price hike.

Fighting terrorism will not succeed as long as a shattering blow has not been delivered against poverty. And this means, first and foremost, unyielding war against corruption, waste, the various forms of pollution, not only of nature, but also natural pollution, on which depends the ability of a society to stand up and launch its development programmes.

Efforts are furnished here and there. But they are still marked by vacillation, by various types of shortcomings and by the resistance of vested interests that are deeply entrenched in society and difficult to uproot.

And yet something is in the making, albeit to take its final shape. Can we benefit from the lessons of the past decades to eradicate poverty and terrorism, or shall we passively accept our fate and let terrorism get the upper hand?

The War Between Israel and Lebanon Was an Oil War

Joel Bainerman

Joel Bainerman is a researcher and frequent commentator on Middle East politics. In the following viewpoint, he explores the theory of Michel Chossudovsky, who argues that the war between Israel and Lebanon in 2006 was precipitated by America's geostrategic goals and the desire to protect the Baku-Tbilisi-Ceyhan (BTC) oil pipeline for the benefit of Israel.

As you read, consider the following questions:

1. What does the BTC oil pipeline bypass, according to the viewpoint?
2. What are the benefits of the BTC oil pipeline for Israel, according to the author?
3. According to the author, how does the BTC oil pipeline affect Israel-Russian relations?

Could the war in Lebanon have been more about protecting oil pipelines and America's geostrategic goals than Hezbollah [Islamist organization based in Lebanon] shooting rockets into northern Israel?

A Canadian economics professor thinks so.

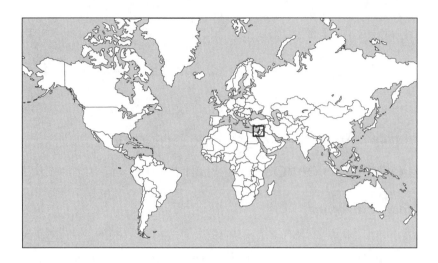

The BTC Pipeline

The inauguration of the Baku-Tbilisi-Ceyhan (BTC) oil pipeline, which links the Caspian Sea to the Eastern Mediterranean, took place on the 13th of July [2006], the day after the war began. Michel Chossudovsky, of the University of Ottawa and director of the Centre for Research on Globalization, reports that just one day before the Israeli air strikes, the main partners and shareholders of the BTC pipeline project, including several heads of state and oil company executives were in attendance at the port of Ceyhan for a reception hosted by Turkey's President Ahmet Necdet Sezer. Among the invited guests BP's [formerly British Petroleum] CEO, Lord Browne, and senior government officials from Britain, the United States and Israel, including Minister of Energy and Infrastructure Binyamin Ben-Eliezer.

BP heads the BTC pipeline consortium. Other major shareholders include Chevron, ConocoPhillips, France's Total and Italy's Eni.

Chossudovsky points out that what is so important about the BTC pipeline it that it bypasses the territory of the Russian Federation. It transits through the former Soviet republics of Azerbaijan and Georgia, both of which have become

US "protectorates", who are already in a military alliance with the United States and NATO [North Atlantic Treaty Organization]. Azerbaijan and Georgia have deep military cooperation agreements with Israel.

"I believe that there are strategic objectives underlying the Lebanon war which are tied to oil and oil pipelines," Chossudovsky says. "By bypassing Russia, Russia has been weakened. Now, Israel is slated to play a major strategic role in 'protecting' the Eastern Mediterranean transport and pipeline corridors out of Ceyhan. Also, Israel will increase dramatically the import of oil from the Caspian Sea for its local economy."

Oil Interests Reign

Chossudovsky, whose international best seller *The Globalization of Poverty* has been published in eleven languages, insists that the bombing of Lebanon was part of a carefully planned and coordinated military road map and that the next stage of the war which would include attacks against Iran and Syria—which he says will be done on behalf of oil interests—not because of any need to safeguard the stability of the region.

"The end result is Israeli territorial control over the East Mediterranean coastline. With this pipeline, the Eastern Mediterranean will now have an 'energy corridor' to the Caspian Sea basin. What is important to remember is that all of the participants in the pipeline are US allies—including Israel, Turkey, Georgia, and Azerbaijan."

"The bombing of Lebanon was part of a carefully planned and coordinated military road map."

For Israel, Chossudovsky's conclusions are chilling: Israel is now part of what he says is "an Anglo-American military axis which serves the interests of the Western oil giants in the Middle East and Central Asia." And yet the Israeli public has no idea that these aims are what might have motivated its government. Most Israelis believed that the IDF [Israeli Defense Forces] tried to do what they could in order to safeguard the security of the Israeli public—and simply failed. Didn't do the job right.

One might even conclude that the plan could have involved Israel being weakened (we couldn't have been any worse—could we?)—so that Hezbollah can score a victory of some sort and thus keep not only southern Lebanon unstable for years to come but much of northwestern Lebanon and southwestern Syria along the Mediterranean coastline.

Think of this in the same way that the Oslo Accords strengthened the Palestinians—while weakening Israel—and led to ten years of unprecedented instability in Israel. The same future may have been deemed for Lebanon with the recent war just the first act in the play. The end result will likely be the United States insisting that its Israeli troops be stationed along this shoreline—not to protect the pipeline—but to "ensure regional stability".

"There are huge rewards for Israel."

Huge Rewards for Israel

This is terrible because the Israeli public will be duped into providing the security and protection for a private pipeline deal? Well, not really. There are huge rewards for Israel.

The BTC pipeline will channel oil to Western markets via an underwater Israeli-Turkish pipeline that will link Ceyhan in Turkey to the Israeli port of Ashkelon (a distance of 400 km) and then through an existing pipeline between Ashkelon and Eilat which was shut down in the late 70s after the fall of the shah and the loss of Iranian oil. Israel will undoubtedly collect some fee on each barrel of oil that is transhipped over its territory on the way to foreign markets.

Militarization of the Eastern Mediterranean

The bombing of Lebanon is part of a carefully planned and coordinated military road map. The extension of the war into Syria and Iran has already been contemplated by U.S. and Israeli military planners. This broader military agenda is intimately related to strategic oil and oil pipelines. It is supported by the Western oil giants which control the pipeline corridors. In the context of the war on Lebanon, it seeks Israeli territorial control over the East Mediterranean coastline.

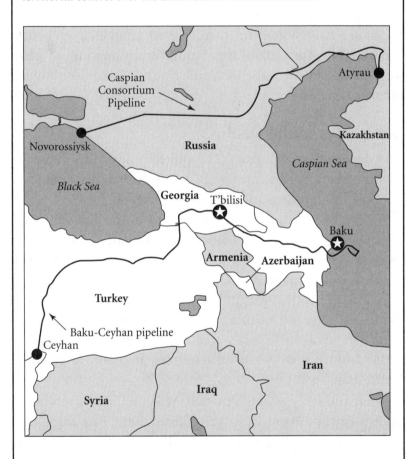

TAKEN FROM: Michel Chossudovsky, "The War on Lebanon and the Battle for Oil," *GlobalResearch.ca,* July 26, 2006.

As it can be assumed the price of oil will continue to rise—if Israel can be guaranteed a reasonable price for its oil and gas in the way of a 30–50-year supply contract—it would not only make the cost of acquiring Israel's energy resources much cheaper and efficient, but also Israeli energy and economic planners could plan, decades in advance, for Israel's hydrocarbon needs.

Also involved in this project is a pipeline to bring water to Israel, pumping from upstream resources of the Tigris and Euphrates river system in Anatolia—yet another huge benefit for Israel. In April 2006, Israel and Turkey announced plans for four underwater pipelines, which would bypass Syrian and Lebanese territory

Downsides of the Deal

The downside of the deal? The pipeline deal directly assails Russian interests at a time when Israel-Russian economic and political relations are warming and deepening.

"Diverting central Asian oil and gas to the Eastern Mediterranean under Israeli military protection, for re-export back to Asia, serves to undermine the inter-Asian energy market, which is based on the development of direct pipeline corridors linking central Asia and Russia to south Asia, China and the Far East," says Chossudovsky. "Ultimately, this design is intended to weaken Russia's role in central Asia and cut off China from central Asian oil resources. It is also intended to isolate Iran."

Chossudovsky points out that Moscow has responded to the US-Israeli-Turkish design to militarize the East Mediterranean coastline with plans to establish a Russian naval base in the Syrian port of Tartus. Moscow also intends to deploy an air defense system around the base to provide air cover for the base itself and a substantial part of Syrian territory.

"Moreover, Moscow and Damascus have reached an agreement on the modernization of Syria's air defenses as well as a program in support to its ground forces, the modernization of its MIG-29 fighters as well as its submarines (as was reported in *Kommersant*, on 2 June 2006). In the context of an escalating conflict, these developments have far-reaching implications."

Chossudovsky points out that these underwater pipeline routes do not overtly encroach on the territorial sovereignty of Lebanon and Syria. On the other hand, the development of alternative land-based corridors (for oil and water) through Lebanon and Syria would require Israeli-Turkish territorial control over the Eastern Mediterranean coastline through Lebanon and Syria.

"The implementation of a land-based corridor, as opposed to the underwater pipeline project, would require the militarization of the East Mediterranean coastline, extending from the port of Ceyhan across Syria and Lebanon to the Lebanese-Israeli border. Is this not one of the hidden objectives of the war on Lebanon? Open up a space which enables Israel to control a vast territory extending from the Lebanese border through Syria to Turkey?"

The Venezuelan Oil Supply Shapes Politics and Culture

Gregory Wilpert

Gregory Wilpert is a German-American sociologist who now teaches in Venezuela. In the following viewpoint, he offers an analysis of the economic, cultural, and political impact of Venezuela's oil industry. Wilpert also chronicles the opposition to oil industry reforms and examines how the government has reacted to the debate over reform.

As you read, consider the following questions:

1. What is "Dutch disease," as described by the author?
2. As cited in the viewpoint, how did Venezuela's 1996 per capita income compare to the 1960 figure?
3. What was the "Organic Law of Hydrocarbons," according to the author?

Perhaps the most important thing to know about Venezuela is that it is an oil-exporting country, the fifth largest in the world, with the largest reserves of conventional oil (light and heavy crude) in the Western Hemisphere and the largest reserves of nonconventional oil (extra-heavy crude) in the world. This fact is of immense importance to understanding Venezuela because it has shaped practically every aspect of the country, its history, its economy, its politics, and its culture. In

Gregory Wilpert, "The Economics, Culture, and Politics of Oil in Venezuela," Venezuelanalysis.com, August 30, 2003. Reproduced by permission.

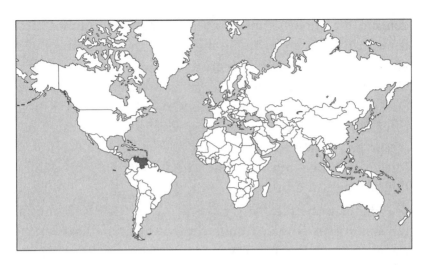

what follows I will provide a brief history of Venezuela's oil industry. Next, I discuss how the oil industry has shaped the economy, polity, and culture. Then, I examine the criticisms leveled against the oil industry and how the [Hugo] Chávez government has proposed to address these. Finally, I present what the opposition has done to prevent the reform of the oil industry and how the government has reacted towards this opposition. . . .

HOW OIL SHAPED VENEZUELAN SOCIETY

Economically

Perhaps the most evident effect oil has had on Venezuela's economy is the appearance of the "Dutch disease." This economic disease is caught whenever a commodity brings a sudden increase of income in one sector of the economy, which is not matched by increased income in other sectors of the economy. What happens is that this sudden sectoral increase causes severe problems in the other sectors. The increased sectoral income causes a distorted growth in services and other non-tradables, which cannot be imported, while discouraging the production of tradables, which are imported. The reason for this disparity is that the greater income rapidly raises the demand for imports, since domestic production cannot meet demand quickly enough, and also raises the demand for services, which the domestic market has to supply because services cannot be imported as easily as tradables can. The increased demand for imported goods and domestic services, in turn, causes an increase in prices, which ought to cause domestic production to increase, but doesn't because the flow of foreign exchange into the economy has caused a general inflation of wages and prices.

One can observe the symptoms of the Dutch disease in the Venezuelan economy quite clearly, when one looks at the extent to which the increase in oil production and income was followed by a corresponding decrease in agricultural production delaying industrialization. While agricultural production made up about one-third of Venezuela's GDP [gross domestic product] in the 1920s, it shrank to less than one-tenth by the 1950s. Currently agriculture makes up about 6% of GDP. Also, industrial production declined between 1990 and 1999 from 50% of GDP to 24% (compared to all of Latin America, which declined from 36% to 29% in the same period). The other Dutch disease symptoms are evident in the constant devaluations of the currency and subsequent inflation which have existed in Venezuela's economy ever since the oil booms of the late 70s and early 80s.

In addition to the typical Dutch disease problem, the sudden increase of oil revenues in Venezuela caused a serious problem in the government's fiscal policies. That is, the new revenues caused the illusion that the oil income could be used to industrialize the country via massive infrastructure projects, to "sow the oil," as the president at the time of the oil boom, Carlos Andrés Pérez, used to say. What happened was that the quadrupled government income caused government spending to quickly increase and even surpass the newfound revenues. When the oil income began to decline again, it was not as easy to reduce government spending as it had been to increase it. The result was that the government gradually went deeper and deeper into debt. Between 1970 and 1994, foreign debt rose from 9% to 53% of GNP [gross national product]. So, as was already stated earlier, while oil prices and revenues declined, so did per capita income and the Venezuelan economy as a whole, and poverty increased. In 1996 Venezuela was one of the very few countries in the world where per capita income was lower than it was in 1960.

"The sudden increase of oil revenues in Venezuela caused a serious problem in the government's fiscal policies."

Culturally

Perhaps the most visible consequence of Venezuela's reliance on oil is that it has fostered a rentier and clientelistic mentality among Venezuelans. That is, the oil wealth has promoted the idea that one can do well in Venezuela, as long as one has access to the country's oil wealth. The consequence was that rather than engaging in creative entrepreneurial activity, Venezuelans were encouraged to ally themselves with the state, seeking either employment or contracts from the state, which had a monopoly on Venezuela's oil income. Political analyst Terry Lynn Karl describes the consequences of oil as follows:

> In the manner of a petro-state, rent seeking had become the central organizing principle of [Venezuela's] political and economic life, and the ossified political institutions in existence operated primarily to perpetuate an entrenched spoils system. Both state agencies and political parties had given up their programmatic roles to become machines for extracting rents from the public arena.

Another observer of Venezuela, the cultural anthropologist Fernando Coronil, argues that Venezuela's oil wealth, which is concentrated in the state, has caused the state to appear to have magical powers, to be able to accomplish just about any feat at no cost to the population.

Thus transformed into a petro-state, the Venezuelan state came to hold the monopoly not only of violence, but of the nation's natural wealth. The state has exercised this monopoly dramaturgically, seeking compliance through the spectacular display of its imperious presence—it seeks to conquer rather than persuade. . . . By manufacturing dazzling development projects that engender collective fantasies of progress, it casts its spell over audiences and performers alike. As a "magnanimous sorcerer," the state seizes its subjects by inducing a condition or state of being receptive to its illusions—a magical state.

Politically

Venezuela's oil economy and culture of course also left a mark on its politics. As a natural consequence of the clientelistic and magical nature of the state was that the state would become very bureaucratic. It is estimated that of the people employed in the formal economy (about 50% of the total working population), approximately 45% are employed through the government.

Another consequence that Venezuela's oil wealth has had for its political system is that it turned it into what political scientist Terry Lynn Karl calls a "pacted democracy." The term pacted democracy describes a democracy which is held together via an agreement among different elite groups. It is a kind of truce among opposing powerful interest groups in the society, so as to maintain their privileges. In Venezuela this truce took the form of the pact of "Punto Fijo," where all major parties were guaranteed access to power in proportion to the voting results. In other words, even if one party won the presidential and legislative elections, it would still be obliged to share the spoils of Venezuela's oil economy among the other parties, more or less according to the vote results. This way each of the main parties (primarily Acción Democratica and Copei) was guaranteed access to jobs, contracts, ministries, etc. To further minimize conflict, the main union federation, CTV, was similarly divided among the parties, although Acción Democratica, as its founder, always was in control of it. Radical socialist and Communist parties were completely excluded from this pact. The pact of Punto Fijo, however, began falling apart once oil rents began to decline in the mid-80s. It then received its deathblow when Hugo Chávez was elected president in 1998.

In terms of Venezuela's level of bureaucratization, the "pacted" nature of its democracy, and the degree of clientelism, Venezuela in many ways resembled one-party state socialist regimes, except that it was governed by an alternating two-party system. Oddly enough, the system neared its end in the same year Eastern Europe's did, in 1989, with the "Caracazo," when there was a general uprising and riots against IMF-mandated [International Monetary Fund-mandated] economic reforms. . . .

OIL INDUSTRY REFORM UNDER CHÁVEZ

Venezuela's oil industry reform encompasses four main areas: solidification of state ownership of the oil industry, tax reform, subordination of the oil industry to national interests, and the strengthening of OPEC [Organization of the Petroleum Exporting Countries].

State Ownership

The 1999 constitution, which was written by Chávez's supporters, anchors state ownership of Venezuela's oil industry in the constitution. It is well known that the government of Rafael Caldera, Chávez's immediate predecessor in the presidency, wanted to privatize PDVSA [Petróleos de Venezuela, S.A.] The new constitution, however, clearly states that "for reasons of economic and political sovereignty and of national strategy, the state will maintain the totality of the shares of PDVSA or of the entity created to manage the oil industry. . . ." In some ways, this article of the constitution was supposed to

153

America's Relationship to and Reliance on Venezuelan Oil

Most of Venezuela's crude oil that is not consumed domestically in Venezuela is exported to the United States. The United States is a natural market for Venezuelan oil because it is so close—about 5 days by tanker to the U.S. Gulf Coast compared to about 30 to 40 days for supplies coming from the Middle East. Moreover, Venezuela's national oil company, Petróleos de Venezuela, S.A. (PDVSA), wholly owns five refineries in the United States and partly owns four other refineries in the United States and U.S. Virgin Islands, either through partnerships with U.S. companies or through PDVSA's U.S. subsidiary, CITGO.

Political strife within Venezuela and political tension between Venezuela and the United States have caused concern about the stability of Venezuelan oil production and exports to the United States. The election of Hugo Chávez as president of Venezuela in 1998 signaled a major change in how the Venezuelan government views the country's oil industry. For example, the government took steps to shift managerial authority for Venezuela's oil resources from PDVSA to the Venezuelan Ministry of Energy and Petroleum. . . . Opposition to the new government culminated in a general strike that lasted from December 2, 2002, until February 2, 2003, and virtually shut down the oil sector of the economy. This strike temporarily decreased world oil supplies by over 2.5 million barrels per day, or about 3.3 percent of total world daily oil supply, and reduced oil exports to the United States by over 1.2 million barrels per day—equivalent to about 11 percent of total U.S. oil imports at the time.

U.S. Government Accountability Office,
U.S. Energy Security: Issues Related to Potential Reductions
in Venezuelan Oil Production, *June 2006.*

mark a definitive break from neo-liberal economic policies that PDVSA had been pursuing prior to Chávez's election.

However, some critics say that a backdoor to privatization remains open because the constitution also says that the state shall own all shares of PDVSA, "except those of subsidiaries, strategic associations, businesses, and whatever other that has constituted or constitutes PDVSA as a result of the development of its business." In other words, in theory, PDVSA could turn its various activities into subsidiaries and then sell them off, one by one. Following the December '02 to January '03 oil industry strike, this is what PDVSA's directors have been considering, mostly in order to rid itself of unprofitable subsidiaries or activities.

Related to state ownership is a provision in the hydrocarbons law which specifies that all state activity related to oil exploration and production is to be dedicated to the "pubic interest." More specifically, it states that all oil related activity must be oriented to support "the organic, integrated, and sustainable development of the country, paying attention to the rational use of resources and the preservation of the environment." Income derived from oil "for the most part" must be used to finance health care, education, and the FIEM (the fund for macroeconomic stabilization, a governmental savings fund).

Tax Reform

The next major target for reform is the way that the Venezuelan government extracts revenue from the oil industry. Here the government introduced a change in the taxation of the oil industry. Since 1943 the government required a royalty payment of 16.6% for every barrel of oil that either PDVSA or a foreign company extracted. In many cases this royalty had even been negotiated to drop to 1% of some foreign investors. A new oil reform that PDVSA was working on in 1998 even suggested eliminating royalty payments entirely. With the new oil reform law of 2001, however, royalty payments were nearly doubled to 30% of the price at which every barrel is sold. At the same time, the government lowered the income tax levied on oil extraction from 67.6% to 50%.

When the government introduced this change, the opposition cried out that the doubling of royalty payments would ruin Venezuela's cooperation with foreign investors and would practically eliminate foreign direct investment in Venezuela. The government's main argument for increasing the royalty payments is based on the fact that it is much easier for the government to collect royalty payments than it is to collect taxes on oil income. That is, the government can track very easily how much oil is being extracted and what the royalty payments should be based on the current price of oil. However, taxes based on oil income are much more difficult to control because PDVSA or other oil companies deduct their expenses from the income on which they have to pay the taxes. Since expenses are not that easily identifiable for an outside auditor, the taxpayer can attempt to inflate expenses, in order to lower their tax payments. By shifting government revenues from taxes to royalties, the government is basically closing loopholes in the tax collection process.

A second and closely related reason for the change in the oil revenue collection process has to do with PDVSA. Chávez and his supporters have long claimed that PDVSA is providing too little of its revenues to the central government, the company's only shareholder. One way to make the company more efficient would thus be to increase its contribution to the government, regardless of its expenses. That is, by making fewer expenses tax deductible, which is what the shift from income tax to royalties does, the company faces a strong incentive to make its operations more efficient. In other words, a tax which allows the deduction of expenses penalizes the oil producer if production is made more efficient. If, on the other hand, the producer has to contribute just as much to the government, regardless of costs or expenses, the "royalty makes the interests of the natural resource owner [the state] and of the investor coincide."

"It is much easier for the government to collect royalty payments than it is to collect taxes on oil income."

"Re-nationalization"

As mentioned earlier, some critics of PDVSA, such as Carlos Mendoza, have called PDVSA's 1976 privatization "phony." Chávez, in his speeches following the collapse of the December 2002 to January 2003 oil-industry shutdown, has thus referred to the regaining of control over PDVSA as a "re-nationalization." What this regaining of control involves is first and foremost increasing PDVSA's efficiency and profitability, so that the company can transfer a greater share of its revenues to the government treasury. The government plans to increase the company's efficiency through the aforementioned changes in taxation, by selling off unprofitable subsidiaries, and by reorganizing the company into two major geographic subdivisions, PDVSA East and PDVSA West. The details of which subsidiaries will be sold and exactly how the company is to be reorganized are still largely unknown as of this writing.

OPEC

When Chávez first came to power, in February 1999, among his highest priorities was to strengthen OPEC and raise the international price of oil. Oil had dropped to less than $10 per barrel, to a large extent because Venezuela was ignoring its OPEC oil-production quotas during the previous government of Rafael Caldera. Also, non-OPEC members such as Mexico and Russia, were increasing their production considerably, further driving down the price of oil. Chávez immediately put

Alí Rodríguez in charge of the Ministry of Energy and Mines (MEM), which oversees PDVSA and oil policy. Within the new government's first 100 days, Rodríguez visited most OPEC and non-OPEC oil-producing countries and returned with a commitment from most of these countries to reduce production or abide by their OPEC quotas. The price of oil immediately went up, from an average price of $12.28/barrel for 1998 to $17.47/barrel for 1999, one of the largest non-war related increases of the past decade. Later, Chávez and Rodríguez managed to convince OPEC to introduce a price band system, of $22 to $28 per barrel, which OPEC would try to maintain.

The following year, 2000, President Chávez spent much time traveling to both OPEC and non-OPEC countries, to consolidate their commitment to restrained oil production and to convince them to attend the second-ever gathering of OPEC heads of state, to be held in Caracas. On September 27 of 2000, Chávez opened and hosted this second OPEC summit. For the Chávez government, the summit had the following six objectives:

- reestablish a dialogue between Venezuela and its partners in OPEC;

- recuperate the credibility of Venezuela in OPEC;

- strengthen OPEC;

- defend oil prices;

- reassume a leadership position within OPEC; and

- consolidate relations between Venezuela and the Arab/ Islamic world.

Given the strengthened position of OPEC in the world today, it is safe to say that the summit's objectives were largely achieved.

[Ultimately, the renaissance of OPEC could be a large part of what motivated the United States to attack Iraq. That is, if

OPEC had remained as defunct as it was when Chávez came to power, it is quite possible that the Bush administration would never have considered controlling Iraq's oil reserves much of an issue. But with the return of OPEC, the consequent rise in oil prices, and the general lack of control the U.S. government felt in the face of an energy crisis and the attack on the World Trade Center, "breaking OPEC's back" became a top priority.]

Opposition to Oil Industry Reform

As has been noted elsewhere, opposition to the Chávez government did not really gain much momentum until Chávez proposed the 49 "enabling laws" ("leyes habilitante"), among the most important of which was the "Organic Law of Hydrocarbons," which specified the institutional and legal changes for governing Venezuela's oil industry. When the law was made public, the outcry, especially among oil industry executives was immediate.

The opposition declared that the new law would doom Venezuela's oil industry because the higher royalties and the limitations placed on joint ventures would make foreign direct investment completely unattractive. One of the main arguments here is that Venezuela's crude oil is mostly heavy and extra-heavy, a type of crude that is quite expensive to extract from oil fields. The shift from taxes to royalties would mean that companies could deduct substantially fewer expenses from the transfers they are required to make to the government. As a result, the extraction of oil from "marginal fields" (fields which yield less oil) and heavy and extra-heavy crude become much less attractive to foreign investors. To support their argument, the opposition points to the fact that Venezuela's royalties are among the highest in the world.

Another element of critique of the government's oil policy has always been that the constitution prohibits the privatization of PDVSA. While few in Venezuela openly favor privatization, due to the strong nationalist sentiment in the country, many have suggested that Venezuelans would be better off if PDVSA were privatized to the general public, in the sense that all citizens would receive shares of PDVSA that they would then be free to buy and sell on the stock market.

Periodical Bibliography

The following articles have been selected to supplement the diverse views presented in this chapter.

Tamsin Carlisle   "Iraq's Chilly Welcome for Oil Majors," *National*, June 20, 2009.

Mark Doyle   "Two Countries' Contrasting Tales," BBC News, April 4, 2005.

Suzanne Goldenberg   "Thirst for Oil Poses Threat to U.S. National Security, Advisor Says," *Guardian*, October 28, 2009.

David Howell   "Energy Myths and Illusions," *Japan Times*, August 15, 2005.

Steven Kopits   "Energy Policy: U.S vs. China," *E&P*, June 1, 2009.

Tom Maliti   "Chad's Oil Creates More Problems Than It Solves," *Mail & Guardian Online*, April 11, 2006.

Jennie Matthew   "Politics Fuels Tension in Sudan's Oil-Rich Crossroads," *Mail & Guardian Online*, April 2, 2008.

Godwin Nnanna   "The New Face of Nigeria's Oil Industry," *China Dialogue*, November 15, 2006.

Marianela Acuña Ortigoza   "Colombia-Venezuela Relations: Between Politics and the Economy," Venezuelanalysis.com, August 13, 2009.

Rob Sherwin   "Hearts and Minds as Important as Oil Finds," *National*, September 17, 2009.

Michael Voss   "Cuba and Venezuela: Oil and Politics," BBC News, December 22, 2007.

Andrew Yorke   "Promise Tempered by Politics," *E&P*, September 1, 2003.

CHAPTER 4

Drilling for New Sources of Oil

Global Drilling Trends and Innovations

Guy Woodall

Guy Woodall is the secretary of the European Drilling Engineering Association and an associate director of OTM Consulting Ltd, a technology management consultancy. In the following viewpoint, he notes the shift toward cost savings in research & development departments, which has huge ramifications in oil-drilling technology. Woodall also emphasizes the value in the collaboration between oil companies and technology developers, as well as competing oil companies, to develop game-changing technological advances to benefit oil companies.

As you read, consider the following questions:

1. According to Woodall, how does a reduction in the overall technology budget of most major oil companies affect drilling innovation?

2. What are the two trends that Woodall has noticed in his role at the European Drilling Engineering Association?

3. What is the main point at which many promising technologies founder, according to Woodall?

Over the last decade, there has been a shift in the structure of the oil and gas industry, which has had a huge effect on the nature of innovation and on how research and development (R&D) is carried out within the industry. Many industry observers will acknowledge that oil companies, the ultimate customers for the whole oil and gas supply chain, are becoming increasingly focused on cost savings. The ramifications for innovation and R&D are as follows.

- A reduction in the overall technology budget of most major oil companies—As fields with marginal economics (small accumulations and brownfields, etc.) compete with 'elephant' fields (huge oil fields) for the resources of Western oil companies, and there is increasing emphasis on environments requiring high technology such as deep water, there is a strong argument that only new technology can benefit oil companies by reducing the per-barrel cost of producing oil. In practice, however, R&D budgets are often among the first to be cut. This leads to a knock-on effect down the supply chain, with all levels becoming cash-starved.

- An increased tendency for oil companies to focus on their core activities and outsource non-core functions—Many see R&D as non-core, hence the amount of R&D being carried out by the oil companies themselves is a fraction of what it was a decade ago. This research is either not being carried out at all, or is divested to large service companies and contractors, many of whom have entered into wide-ranging frame agreements with the oil company. This has had the effect of disenfranchising smaller suppliers and technology development companies from their ultimate customers. Since such small and medium-sized enterprises (SMEs) are a rich source of innovation, the pressure on them is to the detriment of the entire industry.

Technology Management in the Drilling Sector

In recent years, the European Drilling Engineering Association (DEA(E)) has observed the emergence of two significant trends that appear to be mutually reinforcing. The first is the shortage of high-quality technology development project proposals being made to the DEA(E), and the second is the decrease in the proportion of projects that are presented to the DEA(E) that are subsequently sponsored by member oil companies. Although these effects are mutually reinforcing, neither is a direct result of the other; rather, both are a direct result of the decrease in R&D budgets and of the changing dynamics within the industry, whereby innovative SMEs are sidelined, as far as technology development is concerned, by the tendency of oil companies to outsource a range of functions to 'one-stop-shop' providers.

There is a need to stimulate innovation within the industry supply base. Both operators and service companies need to be proactive in this respect; to do nothing within the context of the current industry dynamics between the operators, service companies, contractors and SME suppliers would be to allow innovative talent to be stifled. R&D effort should be focused on the key requirements of the industry, rather than allowing suppliers to commit resources to ideas for which there may be no market. Other ways in which operators and service companies can assist SMEs within the supply base is through direct funding of high-priority development projects and mentoring schemes; running interaction events; developing strategic partnerships with key, highly innovative suppliers; and catalysing collaboration between companies.

As well as encouraging collaboration between technology developers, oil companies themselves can collaborate in the development of important technology for which they all have a need. Joint industry projects (JIPs) ensure that funds committed by the participants are leveraged by the funds of the other participants, ensuring that R&D budgets go further and that effort is not duplicated. Again, operators and service companies can help in identifying both the common technology requirements and the oil companies that may be interested in forming a consortium to sponsor the research.

"The development and deployment of technology is something that cannot be taken for granted."

Addressing Bottlenecks

The main point at which many promising technologies founder is at the field trial stage. Many oil companies admit to just following technology and to being reluctant to be the first to apply an expensive new technology. While they may agree to contribute funding to a JIP, when the product reaches prototype and it is time to trial it, it is often difficult to find a host asset. This 'bottleneck' is a serious impediment to the application of technology that could result in substantial cost savings for the industry.

To mitigate the problem, there are two issues that need to be addressed. First is how to overcome the risk associated with applying a new technology for the first time. More often than not, when it comes to trialling new technology, the deterrent to an asset is not the cost of the technology itself, but the cost if it fails; the worst-case scenario being lost production caused by equipment breaking down in a well. The cost of such lost production would exceed the cost of the technology itself. The second issue is how to match technology at prototype stage and in need of field trial with an asset that has the capability and the incentive to do so.

Therefore, the development and deployment of technology is something that cannot be taken for granted. Operators and service companies and public sector organisations need to be proactive in developing and sponsoring initiatives that can fa-

"They're still using that greasy kid stuff."

"They're still using that greasy kid stuff," cartoon by Vahan Shirvanian. www.Cartoon Stock.com. Copyright © Vahan Shirvanian. Reproduction rights obtainable from www.CartoonStock.com.

cilitate the process. It is also important that companies at every level of the oil and gas supply chain adopt a strategic approach to technology. Such an approach should start with the formulation of an explicit technology strategy that should be coordinated closely with corporate business strategy. It should then go through a number of stages such as the identification and prioritisation of technology needs, sourcing and acquiring the technology (be it through licensing, internal development or outsourcing), applying the technology and learning lessons from the process.

Drilling Technology

Each year, DEA(E) members are asked to vote for the issues that they consider to be of highest importance to them in their daily operations. These issues then become the topics for discussion at the following year's meetings. The results of the voting provide a useful indication of the key challenges facing the drilling sector.

For 2000–2002, the results of the voting are as follows, in priority order:

- expandable casing technology;

- high-pressure/high-temperature wells;

- underbalanced drilling;

- extended reach technology;

- multilateral drilling/completions;

- performance enhancement and measurement;

- deepwater operations;

- low-cost wells; and

- water-based mud versus oil-based mud.

Expandable casing technology was by far the most popular choice, despite the fact that it did not even appear on the list of topics in 2000, so [it] gained all its votes in the last two years. The interest in this technology area reflects the fact that mono-diameter wells, or rather the incremental stages that are gradually being conquered as the industry approaches the ability to drill mono-diameter wells, can increase production, increase reserves and lower costs simultaneously.

None of these, however, can truly be seen as a revolutionary technology; none will fundamentally alter the way in which oil companies and drilling contractors carry out their business. They are evolutionary to the extent that they are advanced forms of the drilling methods carried out many years ago. The technology that does come close—expandable casing—was first mooted over a decade ago and has taken until now to become a reality. One of the key issues facing the industry today is how to encourage innovation so that revolutionary technologies can be conceived and developed that will make changes in the way we drill, enabling us to continue to produce hydrocarbons economically in the coming decades.

Norway's Arctic Oil Exploration Faces Opposition

Gwladys Fouché

Gwladys Fouché writes about the Nordic countries for the Guardian *and other media outlets. In the following viewpoint, she notes that the picturesque Lofoten Islands off the coast of Norway, which could hold 20 percent of the region's undiscovered oil reserves, has become the center of controversy as the local fishing and tourist industries have raised concerns about development in the area.*

As you read, consider the following questions:

1. According to the author, where are the Lofoten Islands located with respect to the Arctic Circle?
2. What kind of damage has oil surveying done to the local fishing industry, according to the viewpoint?
3. According to Fouché, what was Norway's gross domestic product per capita in 2008?

Perched 200 km [kilometres] north of the Arctic Circle, the Lofoten Islands in Norway paint a picture-perfect image of serenity. High mountains plunge into the sea, villages of brightly painted wooden houses nestle on the shores of sheltered bays, while fishing boats pull gently on their anchors.

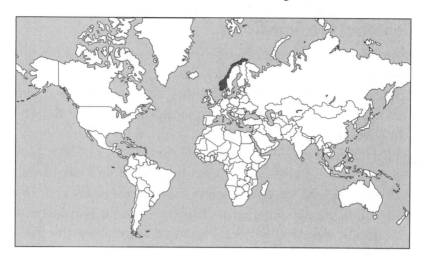

But underneath the surface, the Lofoten Islands are the latest battleground for the right to exploit the polar region's oil and gas resources, with local fishermen and environmentalists hoping to defeat a multibillion pound industry.

As Norway's oil reserves in the North Sea are emptying— the country is the world's fifth largest oil exporter—it is now looking to the Arctic north in search of new oil riches. And the Lofoten Islands appear promising. Between May and September, Norway's state oil agency will be mapping the seabed outside the archipelago in search of hydrocarbon deposits, as it already did in 2008.

"We expect the area to hold 20% of all remaining undiscovered reserves on the Norwegian continental shelf," explained Odd-Ragnar Lorentsen from the Norwegian Petroleum Directorate (NPD).

This view is shared by the oil companies, which are not currently allowed to explore in the region. "There is a potential for oil and gas off the Lofoten," said Ørjan Birkeland, exploration manager for the Norwegian oil company StatoilHydro [Statoil ASA]. "We would like the region to be opened [for drilling]. We must have the ability to explore."

Concerns Are Significant

But not everyone is welcoming a potential oil boom in the region. The fishing industry, which has dominated the economy of the region for the past millennium, fears oil activity could endanger the Barents Sea cod, the largest cod stock in the Atlantic Ocean, which spawns off the coast of Lofoten in February–March and is a highly profitable fishery.

"I am absolutely against searching for oil and gas in the Lofoten area," said a visibly angry Rolf Arne Jacobsen, a 52-year-old fisherman, in the port of Svolvær. "It would be a catastrophic development that would endanger both the fisheries and nature."

"As Norway's oil reserves in the North Sea are emptying . . . it is now looking to the Arctic north in search of new oil riches."

Surveying has already been killing off fish stocks. To map the seabed, scientists shoot out an air pulse at high pressure that rebounds on the seabed, killing any small fish within a 10-metre radius. "The dead fish float on the surface after the surveying ships have done their research," claimed Jacobsen. And it is not known what effects the surveying has on the surviving fish. In some regions, 2008's catches of hake are a tenth of what they were on 2007's—and the fishermen blame the seismic surveys.

Tourist Industry Protest Development

The tourism industry is also up in arms, as Lofoten is one of Norway's top tourist destinations, with travellers flocking to admire its flora and fauna. "Lofoten would be a less attractive destination," said Heike Vester, who runs marine safaris from the port of Henningsvær.

Vester is afraid that oil installations, such as offshore platforms, pipelines and other on-land installations would dam-

No Oil from Lofoten

Oil has made Norway one of the richest countries in the world. But there is no such thing as a risk-free oil production. Some areas should never be exploited. Lofoten is one such area.

WWF Factsheet, *"The Natural Treasures of Lofoten," April 2008.*

age the pristine nature and kill her business. "When I tell my customers what's going on, they tell me they don't want to come back," she said.

Environmentalists also have huge concerns for the fragile Arctic environment. "There are even more storms here than in the North Sea, and during the winter there is only daylight for three to four hours per day [making cleaning operations more difficult]," said Maren Esmark, head of conservation at WWF [World Wildlife Fund] Norway. "An oil spill would have more dramatic consequences, especially since the areas that are being surveyed are very near the coast."

Some Locals Support Development

However, not everyone is opposed to the idea. "We just can't live off tourism and service jobs, we need other types of jobs too," said Brita Malnes, who owns a cornershop in Henningsvær. "If oil and gas mean we could get jobs, then it would be good. But at the same time it should not destroy the nature around here."

Public information meetings for Lofoten's 23,500 inhabitants last year have been tumultuous. "In 30 years of working in the oil industry I have never seen such reactions," said Lorentsen. "At one meeting, a grandmother was in tears because she thought we were going to put her grandson, a fisherman, out of work. . . . People are scared and we should understand that."

Part of Lorentsen's surprise is that this is a country that has grown fabulously wealthy on the oil industry. Thanks to the North Sea's resources, Norway boasts one of the world's largest GDP [gross domestic product] per capita (about $55,669 or £38,242 in 2008, compared with the United Kingdom's $35,070).

North Sea Oil Is Dwindling

But it is precisely the North Sea's declining reserves that are driving the search for oil in the north. Oil production peaked in 2001, and "by 2023, it will have reduced by 50%," said Birkeland. "The way forward is to increase recovery from existing fields and increase exploration."

Already one gas field, Snow White, is being exploited in the Norwegian side of the Barents Sea, with oil companies discovering new fields every year.

StatoilHydro [Statoil ASA] alone has drilled 21 wells and made 14 discoveries. "We made two finds just in 2008," said Birkeland.

Another company, the Italian oil group Eni, is hoping to get the right to exploit the Goliat oil field in the Barents Sea.

Politicians are divided about the way forward. In the cabinet coalition, the Socialist Left Party is opposed to oil exploration around Lofoten, while the dominant partner, Labour, is broadly in favour. Similarly, in opposition, the Christian Democrats and the Liberals oppose it while the Conservatives are in favour. Oil exploration in Lofoten is already set to be one of the top issues of September's general election.

The Norwegian parliament is to decide in 2010 whether to open up Lofoten to oil exploitation. And in the meantime surveying activities off the coast of the archipelago will continue.

Iceland Hopes for Oil Discoveries in the Dragon Zone

Bente Bergøy Miljeteig

Bente Bergøy Miljeteig is a contributor to Norwegian Continental Shelf, *the publication of the Norwegian Petroleum Protectorate. In the following viewpoint, the author reports on the huge oil potential in the Dreki area, also known as the "dragon zone," in northeastern Iceland. Miljeteig describes the hope the small town of Vopnafjordur has for oil exploration and the economic stimulus it will bring.*

As you read, consider the following questions:

1. According to the viewpoint, how many people live in Vopnafjordur?
2. Why are locals so positive about oil exploration, according to council chair Thorsteinn Steinsson?
3. How long is the exploration phase in the Dreki area expected to last, according to the author?

The Dreki (dragon) area opened by the Icelandic authorities for petroleum exploration lies 300 kilometres to the east. In Vopnafjordur, they are waiting for the oil adventure to start.

Bente Bergøy Miljeteig, "Good Base for Expectations," *Norwegian Continental Shelf*, no. 1, 2009. Reproduced by permission.

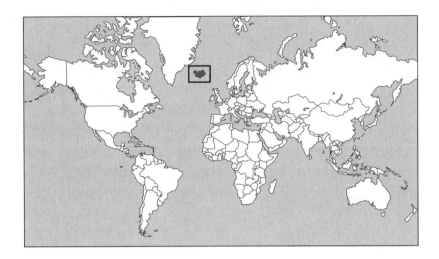

This community in northeastern Iceland is a natural choice for oil companies seeking a base for the continental shelf, maintains council chair Thorsteinn Steinsson.

It lies closest to the Dreki area, he notes, and should accordingly be where the service functions are located—at least during the exploration phase.

He and Magnus M Thorvaldsson, head of administration for the local authority, work in a simple council office building not far from the sea.

Living in Vopnafjordur

Neither boom nor bust in the Icelandic economy has left many visible marks on this coastal community of just over 700 people.

"We've not been much affected by the financial crisis," says Mr Thorvaldsson. "Most people here haven't taken out big loans to buy fine houses and expensive cars. We do well as long as the fishing quotas are good."

A bitter February wind blows over Vopnafjordur. The only visible activity is in the harbour, where seiner *Lundey* is getting ready to sail.

Capelin is being cleaned of roe in the reception plant alongside, and a strong smell of tar and fish pervades the place.

Vopnafjordur lies a three-hour drive along icy, desolate roads through fog and snow from the airport at Egilsstadir, the principal town of eastern Iceland.

About as far from Reykjavik as you can get on land, the area is renowned for its magnificent scenery and good angling rivers. Both President George W Bush and Prince Charles have fished there.

Positive Reaction to Exploration

"Most people here are positive to oil exploration," says Mr Steinsson. "We need more jobs to reduce our dependence on fishing. Vopnafjordur ought to have more legs to stand on."

He believes that natural resources such as fish, geothermal heat, hydropower and possible oil must be exploited—but in an acceptable, long-term and sensible manner.

"The rivers here are so clean that we can drink the water," Mr Steinsson observes. "That's the way we want to keep it."

He explains that the locals are interested in oil exploration, not least after an open meeting in January with Energy Minister Össur Skarphéðinsson (now also foreign minister).

Along with representatives from the National Energy Authority [of Iceland], he gave a briefing on plans and opportunities. Attendance was high.

Vopnafjordur has a number of companies which provide services for the fishing industry, and Mr Steinsson believes that their expertise could be useful for an oil industry supply base.

Roughly 100 people work in the local fishing sector, either at sea or in the processing industry. The HB Grandi plant processes capelin, herring and blue whiting.

Daunting Challenges in Dreki Oil Development

No drilling rigs yet have ventured into the chilly sea region at about 67 degrees north midway between Iceland and Norway. But 8,160 kilometres of seismic surveys suggest the geology might be at least as oil and gas-rich as the Grand Banks of Newfoundland.

The Dreki water temperature averages 0 to 1 degree Celsius. Waves average five to six metres and can be whipped up twice as high. Fog and ice challenge navigation.

The ocean is 1,000 to 1,500 metres deep. Oil and gas deposits are projected to be 3,000 to 3,500 metres beneath the seabed. But Iceland's engineers suggest current oil and gas technology is up to hitting the targets.

Edmonton Journal,
"Northern Reserves Look Tempting," 2008.

Plans to locate an oil base next to the fishing port are seen as a good solution in an impact assessment carried out by consultants Efla Værkfrædistofa and Almenna Verkfrædistofan.

Harbour conditions, water depth and closeness to Dreki are good reasons for choosing Vopnafjordur, this study concluded. It was also considered the cheapest option.

Long Quay Is Needed

According to the assessment, the exploration phase will run for about 10 years and needs a service area of roughly 1.5 to 3 hectares and a quay 100 metres long.

The water depth alongside this quay should be at least 10 metres. A vessel about 80–100 metres long would freight food and technical equipment out to the rigs several times a week.

On its return voyage, this supply ship would carry waste, containers and used equipment. A number of smaller stand-by vessels will be located out by the rigs.

The consultants estimate that roughly 100 people will be employed on each rig, most of them foreigners. They also say that the heliport for crew changes should be at Egilsstadir.

In the event of commercial discoveries, a petroleum receiving and processing facility could be required. That would call for more space and a rather deeper port.

The consultancy report recommends that this should be located at Gunnolfsvik in the neighbouring Langanes local authority, which has some 450 residents.

Big Changes Coming to Vopnafjordur

Messrs Steinsson and Thorvaldsson know that a number of oil companies are interested in exploring the Dreki area, and are likely to have their own views about where a base should lie. The deadline for applications is in May, and things take time.

"If we get this facility, we'll see big changes here," Mr Steinsson acknowledges. "It'll mean new activity, optimism and a lot more jobs.

"Many people moved away to the towns like Akureyri and Reykjavik during the boom times. I hope the trend will now be reversed and bring people back to the districts."

"The local authority is planning how it should deal with a sharp and rapid expansion."

From Fish to Oil

That hope is shared by Sævar Jonsson. A fisherman since 1967, mostly on trawlers, he has been with the *Lundey* seiner in recent years but could fancy a job on an oil service vessel.

"Oil exploration will be good for the country and for Vopnafjordur," he says. "We need jobs, income and educated young people."

If Iceland becomes an oil nation, Mr Jonsson hopes the revenues will be managed in a good way—through a fund, for instance. Coming generations must also benefit.

He says that emigration and an aging population challenge small coastal communities like his own. Only one of his four children lives nearby—the others have moved to town.

Mr Steinsson believes in strong growth, perhaps a doubling in the population. The local authority is planning how it should deal with a sharp and rapid expansion.

The Lure of Vopnafjordur

Vopnafjordur has many qualities which could appeal to people, including a fine and secure place to raise children, a good school and great countryside. Prices are also lower than in town.

Paradoxically, the economic crisis which has hit Iceland could prompt more people to move back to the outlying districts—a positive effect of the collapse.

"Believe me, it was much more fun having a lot of money," says Mr Steinsson with a smile. "But people have a tendency to be more inventive in a downturn. We should have had that creativity when we were rich."

Ghana Gets Ready for Oil Export

Matt Brown

Matt Brown is a contributor to the National, *Abu Dhabi's daily English-language newspaper. In the following viewpoint, he expresses the growing concern that Ghana's newfound oil wealth will generate corruption and conflict. Brown notes that the Ghanaian government is working to make sure that every citizen will benefit from the influx of oil revenue.*

As you read, consider the following questions:

1. According to the viewpoint, how many million barrels of oil do experts estimate are located in the west of Ghana?
2. How much money will that generate every year in oil revenues, as cited by Brown?
3. According to the author, how much of its oil does America intend to obtain from Africa in the next five years?

Here in this gritty port city in eastern Ghana, the country's only oil refinery currently processes 45,000 barrels of crude per day, mostly from other West African countries such

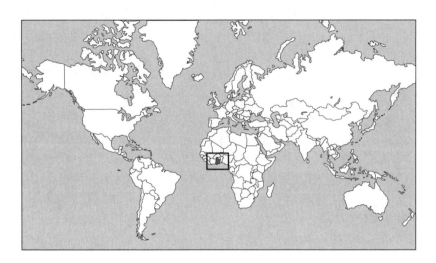

as Nigeria and Angola. But starting next year [2010], the facility could refine Ghanaian crude oil for the first time, creating concern about how the country handles its newfound wealth.

Ghana Is Oil Rich

Ghana is sitting on at least 600 million barrels of oil in offshore fields in the west of the country. That is enough to generate US$1 billion (Dh3.67bn) per year once the oil starts flowing, according to the International Monetary Fund.

Officials here say they are learning lessons from other African oil-producing states, such as Nigeria. Ghana's regional neighbor is one of the most corrupt places on earth, partly because of the country's oil wealth.

Militant groups there, fighting for a cut of the revenue and development in oil-producing regions, frequently sabotage oil installations and kidnap foreign workers.

"We are aware that we need to do things the right way so that our oil becomes a blessing and not a curse," said Michael Sarpong of Ghana's Ministry of Energy.

"We are learning from other countries' challenges and we are trying to put a good system in place."

Oil Revenues Bring Challenges and Temptations

John Atta Mills, the recently elected president, and other members of his social democratic government are working to ensure every Ghanaian benefits from the wealth, Mr Sarpong said.

Ghana has a reputation for transparency in government and is ranked the sixth least corrupt country in Africa by Transparency International, a group that monitors corruption.

However, corruption watchdogs in Ghana warn that its politicians may not be so saint-like when confronted with potential billions of dollars in oil revenue.

"There is a lot of potential for corruption, especially among our politicians," said Vitus Azeem, director of the Ghana Integrity Initiative, the local chapter of Transparency International.

"It means everyone must be alert and keep drawing the public's attention to the issue of corruption, especially once the oil starts pumping," he added.

Tullow, a British oil company, discovered the deep water oil deposits two years ago. Currently, about seven companies own concessions to drill off Ghana's shore, according to the Ministry of Energy.

President Obama's Visit

US President Barack Obama's visit to Ghana last week [July 2009]; his first official trip to Africa, came amid speculation that the United States is trying to manoeuvre for Ghana's oil. But Mr Obama and Mr Mills barely mentioned natural resources in public, and details of their closed-door meeting have not been released.

Mr Mills, a populist president, said Ghana's oil wealth should be used to help the country's development. "Ghanaians

183

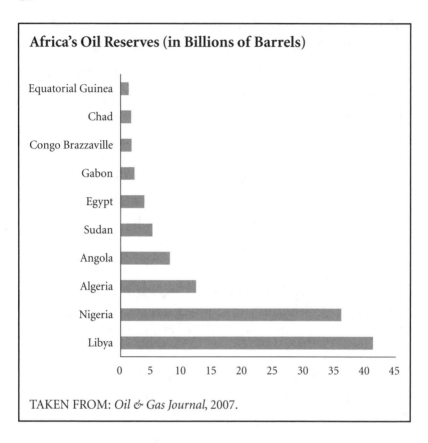

Africa's Oil Reserves (in Billions of Barrels)

TAKEN FROM: *Oil & Gas Journal*, 2007.

expect me to translate the recently discovered oil and gas resources to develop a diverse economy," he told Parliament last week.

For the US's part, it aims to obtain 25 per cent of its oil from Africa in the next five years, according to the National Intelligence Council. The United States currently gets 15 per cent from the continent. With Nigeria's volatile history, Ghana seems to be a logical new source.

In a speech to Ghana's parliament last week, Mr Obama told Ghanaians to use their oil resources wisely. He said Ghana should continue diversifying its economy and not rely on one single export, like the country has done in the past with cocoa.

"Oil brings great opportunities, and you have been very responsible in preparing for new revenue," he said. "But as so many Ghanaians know, oil cannot simply become the new co-coa."

"Ghana's oil wealth should be used to help the country's development."

Ghana Must Use Resources Efficiently

Once Ghana starts pumping oil, it is forecast to produce 100,000 barrels a day, not as much as other West African producers such as Nigeria, Angola, Equatorial Guinea and Gabon, but enough to significantly boost its economy, creating jobs and opportunities for Ghanaians, who are used to living on an average of $2 per day, according to the US State Department.

Ghana is regularly crippled by fuel shortages. The most recent was last week, during Mr Obama's visit, when queues at petrol stations stretched half a kilometre in places.

Ghanaians seem to think pumping their own oil will solve all their fuel security needs, although, ironically, petrol shortages are common in oil-rich countries such as Nigeria, as most oil is exported.

Last week, fishermen in Tema could not go out to sea because there was no fuel for their boats. They believe local leaders, who tell them that Ghana's oil will be the cure to all their problems.

Arctic Oil Exploration Must Not Compromise the Environment

Michael McCarthy

Michael McCarthy is a reporter for the British newspaper the Independent. *In the following viewpoint, he maintains that ever since climate change has opened up wide swaths of the Arctic Ocean, countries are jumping at the chance to develop the region's oil reserves. McCarthy notes the growing environmental concerns about Arctic oil exploration, which assert that any development should protect the region's unique ecosystem and wildlife.*

As you read, consider the following questions:

1. How many billions of barrels of oil does the author estimate are located in the Arctic?
2. According to McCarthy, there are enough undiscovered oil reserves in the Arctic to supply the world for how many years?
3. What five countries, according to the viewpoint, have been actively lobbying to stake a claim on Arctic oil?

The future of the Arctic will be less white wilderness, more black gold, a new report on oil reserves in the High North has signalled this week. The first comprehensive assessment of

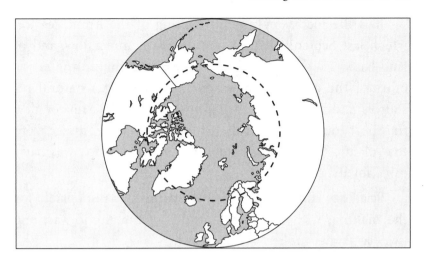

oil and gas resources north of the Arctic Circle, carried out by American geologists, reveals that underneath the ice, the region may contain as much as a fifth of the world's undiscovered yet recoverable oil and natural gas reserves.

This includes 90 billion barrels of oil, enough to supply the world for three years at current consumption rates, or to supply America for 12, and 1,670 trillion cubic feet (tcf) of gas, which is equal to about a third of the world's known gas reserves.

"The first comprehensive assessment of oil and gas resources north of the Arctic Circle ... reveals that underneath the ice, the region may contain as much as a fifth of the world's undiscovered yet recoverable oil and natural gas reserves."

The significance of the report is that it puts firm figures for the first time on the hydrocarbon riches which the five countries surrounding the Arctic—the United States, Russia, Canada, Norway and Denmark (through its dependency, Greenland)—have been eyeing up for several years.

It is the increasingly rapid melting of the Arctic sea ice, which last September hit a new record summer low, and of land-based ice on Greenland, which is opening up the possibility of the once frozen wasteland providing a natural resources and minerals bonanza, not to mention a major new transport route—last year the fabled North-West Passage from the Atlantic to the Pacific along the top of Canada was navigable for the first time.

Scientists consider that global warming is responsible for the melting, with the high latitudes of the Arctic warming twice as fast as the rest of the world.

Environmentalists see this as a massive danger, with the melting of Greenland's land-based ice adding to sea-level rise, while the melting of the sea ice uncovers a dark ocean surface that absorbs far more of the sun's heat than the ice did, and thus acts as a "positive feedback" reinforcing warming. The melting of Greenland's ice sheet has accelerated so dramatically that it is triggering earthquakes for the first time, with movements of gigantic pieces of ice creating shockwaves with a magnitude of up to three.

Conservationists are also concerned about the threat to the Arctic's unique ecosystems and wildlife.

The Arctic countries' governments, on the other hand, see it as a massive opportunity, and are already positioning themselves to claim stakes in the seabed of the Arctic Ocean, if—as many climate scientists now believe will happen—it becomes ice-free in summer within a couple of decades.

Just a year ago, to much media fanfare, the Russians planted a flag on the seabed some 2.5 miles beneath the ice at the North Pole, and dispatched a nuclear-powered icebreaker to map a subsea link between the Pole and Siberia, as part of an effort to circumvent a UN convention limiting resource claims beyond 200 miles offshore.

Melting Arctic Ice

This focus on the Far North comes as a result of the stunningly swift disappearance of ice in the Arctic Ocean. Scientists estimate that summer sea ice has declined by about 50 percent since the 1950s. Last year [2007], summer sea ice extent reached a record low, and thick, multi-year sea ice now covers less than 30 percent of the ocean, down from more than 50 percent in the mid-1980s. Experts who once believed that the Arctic Ocean would not be largely free of summer ice until mid-to-late century now concede that the ice could be gone within a decade.

Ed Struzik,
"The Arctic Resource Rush Is On,"
Yale Environment 360, July 10, 2008.

Canada said earlier this month that it plans to counter the Russian overture with "a very strong claim" to Arctic exploration rights.

This week's oil and gas study carried out by the U.S. Geological Survey, does not raise the national competitive stakes appreciably as it reveals that most of the reserves are lying close to the shore, within the territorial jurisdiction of the countries concerned. Much of the oil is off Alaska; much of the natural gas off the Russian coastline. There appear to be only small reserves under the unclaimed heart of the Arctic.

However, what the report does do is to indicate a very different future for one of the world's last remaining pristine and utterly unspoiled regions. If the oil is there, countries which own it will be very likely to seek to extract it, whatever the environmental cost.

"Before we can make decisions about our future use of oil and gas and related decisions about protecting endangered species, native communities and the health of our planet, we need to know what's out there," said the U.S. Geological Survey's (USGS) director, Mark Myers, in releasing the report. "With this assessment, we're providing the same information to everyone in the world so the global community can make those difficult decisions," he said.

"Most of the Arctic, especially offshore, is essentially unexplored with respect to petroleum," said Donald Gautier, the project chief for the assessment. "The extensive Arctic continental shelves may constitute the geographically largest unexplored prospective area for petroleum remaining on Earth."

"If the oil is there, countries which own it will be very likely to seek to extract it, whatever the environmental cost."

The geologists studied maps of subterranean rock formations across the 8.2 million square miles above the Arctic Circle to find areas with characteristics similar to oil and gas finds in other parts of the world. The study also took into account the age, depth and shape of rock formations in judging whether they are likely to contain oil.

More than half of the undiscovered oil resources are estimated to occur in just three geologic provinces: Arctic Alaska (30 billion barrels), the Amerasia Basin (9.7 billion barrels) and the East Greenland Rift Basins (8.9 billion barrels). More than 70 per cent of the undiscovered natural gas is likely to be in three provinces: the West Siberian Basin (651 tcf), the East Barents Basins (318 tcf) and Arctic Alaska (221 tcf), the USGS said. The study took in all areas north of latitude 66.56 degrees north, and included only reserves that could be tapped using existing techniques. Experimental or unconventional prospects such as oil shale, gas hydrates and coal-bed methane were not included in the assessment.

The 90 billion barrels of oil expected to be in the Arctic in total are more than all the known reserves of Nigeria, Kazakhstan and Mexico combined, and could meet current world oil demand of 86.4 million barrels a day for almost three years. But the Arctic's oil is not intended to replace all the supplies in the rest of world. It would last much longer by boosting available supplies and possibly reducing US reliance on imported crude, if America developed the resources.

The report did not include an estimate for how long it might take to bring the reserves to markets, but it would clearly be a substantial period. Offshore fields in the Gulf of Mexico and West Africa can take a decade or longer to begin pumping oil. But clearly, the massive amount of industrial infrastructure necessary to find the oil, extract it, and transport it to where it is wanted will come with a very considerable environmental cost. Senior US oil executives are urging the relaxation of prohibitions against offshore drilling, including much of Alaska, although Democratic leaders in both houses of Congress rejected President George Bush's effort on 14 July to end a 25-year moratorium on drilling in most coastal waters. But change may well be coming now.

Frank O'Donnell, president of the US environmental group Clean Air Watch, said not only do polar bears and other wildlife within the Arctic Circle face losing their habitat due to global warming, they would be hurt by companies searching for oil. "On the one hand you may see this region more accessible [for getting energy supplies], but we're definitely going to pay a different kind of price ... you may lose species," Mr O'Donnell said. "The oil industry goes up there and industrialises what has been a pristine area ... suddenly it becomes the new Houston."

Staking a Claim

United States. The last country to formally stake its claim will be the first to start large-scale drilling. Thanks to its vast Alaskan territory the United States will be confident of a huge oil bonanza. The White House resisted giving endangered status to the polar bear as long as it could to keep freedom to drill.

Russia. Dramatically upped the stakes in the race for the Arctic last year by planting its flag on the seabed at the magnetic pole with the help of an experimental submarine. The country least likely to baulk at the environmental cost of drilling in the wilderness.

Greenland (Denmark). The island is financially dependent on its mother country, Denmark. Oil could change all that. Its tiny population of 50,000 fears being overrun by outsiders in a future oil rush. Denmark was the first to stake its claim to the North Pole.

Canada. Canada was affronted by Danish claims to the North Pole and has conducted military exercises over its vast northern territories to strengthen its claim to the Arctic. Ottawa has sent naval vessels and specialist troops to the Far North.

Norway. The country does not want to be left out of an Arctic carve-up. But it backs a UN treaty to demilitarise the region and protect its pristine environment.

Periodical Bibliography

The following articles have been selected to supplement the diverse views presented in this chapter.

Tom Davis — "How Research Can Help Oil and Gas Survive Tough Economic Times," *E&P*, February 6, 2009.

Charles Digges — "Russian Arctic Underwater Oil Expedition Reaches North Pole," Environment News Service, August 2, 2007.

Gwynne Dyer — "Eagerly Awaiting a Warmer Arctic," *Japan Times*, May 28, 2008.

Gwynne Dyer — "Is the End of Oil in Sight?" *Japan Times*, December 27, 2008.

Lorrie Goldstein — "Like It or Not, Oilsands Projects Vital," *Ottawa Sun*, September 17, 2009.

Gonzalo Gomez — "Energy Affairs, Technology and Security of State," Venezuelanalysis.com, February 12, 2004.

OilVoice.com — "Vast Exploration Updates Exploration Activities in Kurdistan Region of Iraq," November 3, 2009. www.oilvoice.com.

Bob Peebler — "Advanced Technologies Now More Than Ever," *E&P*, June 2, 2009.

Chris Stanton — "For Oil Firms, Company Culture Is as Important as Drilling Holes," *National*, October 6, 2009.

Melanie Swan — "Meet the Engineers of Tomorrow," *National*, September 29, 2009.

Nick Terdre — "Finding Better Ways to Drill," *Norwegian Continental Shelf*, May 2009.

Times Online — "Russia Warns of War Within a Decade of Arctic Oil and Gas Resources," May 14, 2009.

For Further Discussion

Chapter 1

1. After reading the viewpoints in the chapter, describe how oil production and supply impacts gas prices. How will these factors affect the world economy? Your community?

2. The International Energy Agency calls for an "energy revolution." What does this mean? What forms could such a revolution take?

Chapter 2

1. Noeleen Heyzer outlines the challenges China faces when it comes to environmental issues. Do you think China is fully confronting the threat of global climate change? How can adopting environmentally friendly policies change the way China is perceived worldwide?

2. Stephen Hesse describes how Japan has taken a leadership position regarding energy issues and climate change. What policies can the United States adopt to fight climate change?

Chapter 3

1. William Rees-Mogg discusses how global power is shifting to oil-rich countries. What does Rees-Mogg's analysis mean for the United States? How can the United States remedy the shifting balance of power?

2. Mohamed Sid-Ahmed argues that global oil insecurity is the source of a number of conflicts and is directly related to terrorist activities. What do you think is the relationship between oil and terrorism? How can the United States help to alleviate terrorism?

Chapter 4

1. A recurring theme in this chapter is the tension between oil exploration and development and protection of the natural environment. For example, Michael McCarthy explores the concerns raised over oil exploration in the Arctic. After reading the viewpoints on this topic in the chapter, do you feel that these are well-founded concerns? What issue should be a higher priority for potentially oil-rich regions: economic benefits or environmental protection?

2. Matt Brown examines the way in which Ghana's new-found oil wealth has caused concerns over corruption and exploitation. Are these concerns valid? What are some ways Ghana can avoid conflict and spread the benefits of oil development to all its citizens?

Organizations to Contact

The editors have compiled the following list of organizations concerned with the issues debated in this book. The descriptions are derived from materials provided by the organizations. All have publications or information available for interested readers. The list was compiled on the date of publication of the present volume; the information provided here may change. Be aware that many organizations take several weeks or longer to respond to inquiries, so allow as much time as possible.

African Petroleum Producers' Association (APPA)

1097 Brazzaville
  Democratic Republic of the Congo
(242) 665 38 57
e-mail: appa@appa.int
Web site: www.appa.int

Established in 1987, the African Petroleum Producers' Association (APPA) is an intergovernmental organization that facilitates cooperation and coordination between sixteen oil-producing countries in Africa. APPA disseminates information and promotes projects and policy initiatives that aim to maximize profits and opportunities brought about by oil production. It also offers an up-to-date listing of oil statistics of each member country. APPA publishes the *APPA Bulletin,* a biannual periodical that provides data, information, and news on the organization's activities and the global and regional state of the oil industry. The APPA Web site also features transcripts of recent speeches, seminars, and conferences.

American Petroleum Institute (API)

1220 L Street NW, Washington, DC   20005-4070
(202) 682-8000
Web site: www.api.org

The American Petroleum Institute (API) is a national trade organization that represents approximately four hundred oil

producers, refiners, suppliers, pipeline operators, marine trans-
porters, and service and supply companies. In recent years,
API has grown internationally to advocate for policies that
support the oil industry worldwide. It also offers research on
industry trends, sponsors research ranging from economic
analyses to toxicology, disseminates environmental health and
safety regulations and information, and reports on recent
drilling activities and technological progress. The API provides
certification programs for oil industry professionals as well as
safety, environmental health, and quality control training. API
publishes more than two hundred thousand books, pamphlets,
training and safety manuals, statistical research, and newsletters each year.

Association for the Study of Peak Oil & Gas (ASPO)

Klintvagen 42, Uppsala   SE-765 55
   Sweden
+46 471 00 00
e-mail: mikael.hook@fysast.uu.se
Web site: www.peakoil.net

The Association for the Study of Peak Oil & Gas (ASPO) is a
network of scientists focusing on the study of peak oil and the
economic and scientific consequences of the oil production
decline. ASPO strives to determine an accurate date for the
point of peak oil and to spread awareness of the consequences
of less and less oil on oil-dependent countries. The ASPO
newsletter is published monthly, and the organization offers
statistical information as well as a number of academic theses,
peer-reviewed articles, and books providing valuable insight
into the topic of peak oil on its Web site.

Canadian Association of Petroleum Producers (CAPP)

2100, 350 Seventh Avenue SW, Calgary, Alberta   T2P 3N9
   Canada
(403) 267-1100 • fax: (403) 261-4622
e-mail: communication@capp.ca
Web site: www.capp.ca

The Canadian Association of Petroleum Producers (CAPP) is an association of Canadian companies that works to explore and develop oil and natural gas reserves across Canada. CAPP's associate members offer a broad range of services that support the upstream crude oil and natural gas industry. CAPP strives to foster improvements in the industry's environmental, safety, and health performance while facilitating profits and success in the field. It lobbies for federal and provincial legislation to build a practical and effective regulatory framework. CAPP has compiled wide-ranging statistical information on the Canadian oil and natural gas industry in its *Statistical Handbook*, which can be found on its Web site. It also publishes oil forecasts, comprehensive industry reports, and in-depth studies of relevant issues impacting the Canadian oil and natural gas industry.

Independent Petroleum Association of America (IPAA)

1201 Fifteenth Street NW, Suite 300, Washington, DC 20005
(202) 857-4722 • fax: (202) 857-4799
Web site: www.ipaa.org

The Independent Petroleum Association of America (IPAA) is a national trade association representing independent oil and natural gas producers and service companies that develop 90 percent of domestic oil and gas wells, produce 68 percent of domestic oil, and produce 82 percent of domestic natural gas. IPAA advocates and lobbies for the interests of its members with the U.S. Congress, federal agencies, and the administration. It also researches and provides economic and statistical information about the exploration and development of offshore wells. The IPAA publishes a weekly newsletter, *Washington Report*, which covers legislative and regulatory issues in the industry. The IPAA Web site also offers a broad range of reports and statistical studies covering the oil and gas industry and provides supply-and-demand forecasts.

International Energy Agency (IEA)

9 rue de la Fédération, Paris 75739
France

+33 1 40 57 65 00 • fax: +33 1 40 57 65 59
e-mail: info@iea.org
Web site: www.iea.org

The International Energy Agency (IEA) is an intergovernmental association that advises its twenty-eight member countries on issues of energy policy and clean energy. The IEA focuses on finding solutions for its members on energy security, economic development, and environmental protection, especially on climate change. It conducts energy research and statistical compilation to assess the current state of the energy market and future trends in the industry; disseminates the latest energy news and policy analyses; and provides well-researched recommendations to member states. It publishes numerous in-depth reports offering insight on the energy industry and specific energy topics as well as its monthly newsletter, *IEA OPEN Energy Technology Bulletin*, which provides regular updates on energy security and environmental issues.

International Petroleum Industry Environmental Conservation Association (IPIECA)

5th Floor, 209-215 Blackfriars Road, London   SE1 8NL
  United Kingdom
+44 (020) 7633 2388 • fax: +44 (020) 7633 2389
e-mail: info@ipieca.org
Web site: www.ipieca.org

The International Petroleum Industry Environmental Conservation Association (IPIECA) is an international association that promotes the interests of the oil and gas industry on important global environmental and social issues to the United Nations. IPIECA also fosters cooperation and communication between companies and governments and disseminates information on the latest developments and technological breakthroughs that affect productivity, profitability, safety, and the environment. IPIECA offers a broad range of publications on its Web site, including the *IPIECA Annual Review, Oil and Gas Sector Report Card*, and *IPIECA in Profile*. It also sponsors seminars, conferences, and forums, all of which are listed on its Web site.

Institute for Energy Research (IER)
1100 H Street NW, Suite 400, Washington, DC   20005
(202) 621-2950 • fax: (202) 637-2420
Web site: www.instituteforenergyresearch.org

Founded in 1989, the Institute for Energy Research (IER) is a nonprofit organization that conducts intensive research and analysis on the functions, operations, and government regulation of global energy markets. IER promotes the idea that unfettered energy markets provide the most efficient and effective solutions for today's global energy and environmental challenges and works to educate legislators, policy makers, and the public on the vital role offshore drilling plays in our energy future. IER publishes various fact sheets and comprehensive studies on renewable and nonrenewable energy sources, the growing green economy, climate change, and offshore oil exploration and drilling opportunities. IER also maintains a blog on its Web site that provides timely comment on relevant energy and legislative issues.

Organization of Arab Petroleum Exporting Countries (OAPEC)
PO Box 20501, Safat   13066
   Kuwait
00965-24959000 • fax: 00965-24959755
e-mail: oapec@oapecorg.org
Web site: www.oapecorg.org

The Organization of Arab Petroleum Exporting Countries (OAPEC) is a cartel of eleven Arab and North African countries. OAPEC facilitates the development of the petroleum industry by fostering cooperation among its members and sponsors joint ventures between member states. The organization participates in numerous international meetings, seminars, and regional conferences to advance the interests of Arab oil-producing nations. OAPEC researches and disseminates important statistical information on the global state of the oil market as well as statistics on oil production in member countries in its publication, the *Annual Statistical Bulletin*. It also publishes a quarterly periodical, *Energy Resources Monitor*, which reviews world progress in oil development and drilling. OAPEC also produces a number of books, pamphlets, reports, and conference transcripts.

Organization of the Petroleum Exporting Countries (OPEC)

Helferstorferstrasse 17, Vienna   A-1020
   Austria
Web site: www.opec.org

The Organization of the Petroleum Exporting Countries (OPEC) is a cartel of twelve oil-exporting countries. OPEC countries coordinate their oil production policies in order to stabilize the oil market and ensure profits for oil-producing countries. OPEC publishes *World Oil Outlook*, an annual report on the global state of oil production as well as an annual statistical bulletin. The *OPEC Energy Review* is a quarterly academic journal featuring research articles on energy economics and related issues. The *OPEC Bulletin* is a monthly magazine that covers relevant issues and the state of the world oil market.

Society of Petroleum Engineers (SPE)

222 Palisades Creek Drive, Richardson, TX   75080-2040
(972) 952-9393 • fax: (972) 952-9435
e-mail: spedal@spe.org
Web site: www.spe.org

The Society of Petroleum Engineers (SPE) is an international professional organization for petroleum engineers devoted to collecting, disseminating, and exchanging technical knowledge concerning the exploration, development, and production of oil and gas resources. The SPE supports the development of more efficient and environmentally sound technologies for the public benefit. SPE also offers opportunities for engineers to enhance their technical and professional competence. It publishes a number of scholarly books and reports as well as the monthly publication, *Journal of Petroleum Technology*, which presents authoritative briefs and features on oil and gas industry issues and news about SPE and its members.

Union of Concerned Scientists (UCS)
2 Brattle Square, Cambridge, MA   02238-9105
(617) 547-5552 • fax: (617) 864-9405
Web site: www.ucsusa.org

Founded by scientists and students at Massachusetts Institute of Technology (MIT) in 1969, the Union of Concerned Scientists (UCS) is the leading science-based nonprofit working for a healthy environment and a safer world. UCS utilizes independent scientific research and citizen action to implement innovative solutions and to secure responsible changes in government policy, corporate practices, and consumer choices. UCS publishes in-depth reports on several important issues: global warming, scientific integrity, clean energy and vehicles, global security, and food and agriculture. It also publishes the *Catalyst* magazine, *Earthwise* newsletter, and *Greentips* newsletter.

U.S. Energy Association (USEA)
1300 Pennsylvania Avenue NW, Washington, DC   20004-3022
(202) 312-1230 • fax: (202) 682-1682
e-mail: reply@usea.org
Web site: www.usea.org

The United States Energy Association (USEA) is an association of public and private energy-related organizations, corporations, and government agencies; it promotes the varied interests of the U.S. energy sector by disseminating information about and the understanding of energy issues. In conjunction with the U.S. Agency for International Development and the U.S. Department of Energy, USEA sponsors the Energy Partnership Program as well as numerous policy reports and conferences dealing with global and domestic energy issues. USEA organizes trade and educational exchange visits with other countries and provides information on presidential initiatives, government agencies, and national service organizations.

Bibliography of Books

Bilaal Abdullah   *Peak Oil Paradigm Shift: The Urgent Need for a Sustainable Energy Model.* Trinidad and Tobago: Medianet Limited, 2005.

John Scales Avery   *Energy, Resources and the Long-Term Future.* Hackensack, NJ: World Scientific, 2007.

Gawdat Bahgat   *American Oil Diplomacy in the Persian Gulf and the Caspian Sea.* Gainesville, FL: University of Florida, 2003.

Carolyn Barta   *ENSCO: The First Twenty Years.* Houston, TX: Gulf Publications, 2008.

Nathan J. Citino   *From Arab Nationalism to OPEC: Eisenhower, King Sa'ud, and the Making of U.S.-Saudi Relations.* Bloomington, IN: Indiana University Press, 2002.

Jerome R. Corsi and Craig R. Smith   *Black Gold Stranglehold: The Myth of Scarcity and the Politics of Oil.* Nashville, TN: WND Books, 2005.

Carol A. Dahl   *International Energy Markets: Understanding Pricing, Policies, and Profits.* Tulsa, OK: PennWell, 2004.

Rebecca Harman   *The Earth's Resources.* Chicago, IL: Heinemann Library, 2005.

Mike Heffernan — *Rig: An Oral History of the Ocean Ranger Disaster*. St. John's, Newfoundland: Creative Publishers, 2009.

Dieter Helm, ed. — *The New Energy Paradigm*. Oxford: Oxford University Press, 2007.

Dilip Hiro — *Blood of the Earth: The Battle for the World's Vanishing Oil Resources*. New York: Nation Books, 2007.

Thomas Homer-Dixon, ed. — *Carbon Shift: How the Twin Crises of Oil Depletion and Climate Change Will Change the Future*. Toronto: Random House Canada, 2009.

Philippe Le Billon, ed. — *The Geopolitics of Resource Wars: Resource Dependence, Governance and Violence*. London: Frank Cass, 2005.

Peter M. Lewis — *Growing Apart: Oil, Politics, and Economic Change in Indonesia and Nigeria*. Ann Arbor, MI: University of Michigan Press, 2007.

Daniel Moran and James A. Russell, eds. — *Energy Security and Global Politics: The Militarization of Resource Management*. New York: Routledge, 2008.

Craig Morris — *Energy Switch: Proven Solutions for a Renewable Future*. Gabriola Island, British Columbia: New Society Publishers, 2006.

Sheila Newman, ed. — *The Final Energy Crisis*. London: Pluto Press, 2008.

Peter R. Odell — *Why Carbon Fuels Will Dominate the 21st Century's Global Energy Economy.* Brentwood, England: Multi-Science Publications, 2004.

Chris Oxlade — *How We Use Oil.* Chicago, IL: Raintree, 2004.

Francisco Parra — *Oil Politics: A Modern History of Petroleum.* New York: I.B. Tauris, 2004.

John T. Perry, ed. — *Energy Prices: Supply, Demand, or Speculation?* Hauppauge, NY: Nova Science Publishers, 2009.

Dale Allen Pfeiffer — *Eating Fossil Fuels: Oil, Food, and the Coming Crisis in Agriculture.* Gabriola Island, British Columbia: New Society Publishers, 2006.

Paul Roberts — *The End of Oil: On the Edge of a Perilous New World.* Boston, MA: Houghton Mifflin, 2005.

Hope E. Robertson — *Focusing on the Demand Side of the Power Equation: Implications and Opportunities.* Cambridge, MA: CERA, 2006.

Julia Ruggeri — *Life Offshore.* Austin, TX: Petroleum Extension Service, University of Texas at Austin, 2007.

Matt Savinar — *The Oil Age Is Over: What to Expect as the World Runs Out of Cheap Oil, 2005–2050.* Santa Rosa, CA: Savinar Publishing, 2004.

Toby Shelley   *Oil: Politics, Poverty, and the Planet.* New York: Zed Publishing, 2005.

Jill Sherman   *Oil and Energy Alternatives.* Edina, MN: ABDO Publishing Company, 2009.

Max Siollun   *Oil, Politics and Violence: Nigeria's Military Coup Culture.* New York: Algora, 2009.

Benjamin Smith   *Hard Times in the Lands of Plenty: Oil Politics in Iran and Indonesia.* Ithaca, NY: Cornell University Press, 2007.

Denise Walker   *Fuel and the Environment.* North Mankato, MN: Smart Apple Media, 2008.

Index

Geographic headings and page numbers in **boldface** refer to viewpoints about that country or region.